The Open University

Block 6

Nations and Imperialism 1870–1900

Donna Loftus, Robin Mackie and Annika Mombauer

Course Conclusion

Bernard Waites

D1419896

This publication forms part of an Open University course *A200 Exploring History: Medieval to Modern 1400–1900.*. Details of this and other Open University courses can be obtained from the Student Registration and Enquiry Service, The Open University, PO Box 197, Milton Keynes, MK7 6BJ, United Kingdom: tel. +44 (0)870 333 4340, email general-enquiries@open.ac.uk

Alternatively, you may visit the Open University website at http://www.open.ac.uk where you can learn more about the wide range of courses and packs offered at all levels by The Open University.

To purchase a selection of Open University course materials visit http://www.ouw.co.uk, or contact Open University Worldwide, Michael Young Building, Walton Hall, Milton Keynes MK7 6AA, United Kingdom for a brochure. tel. +44 (0)1908 858785; fax +44 (0)1908 858787; email ouwenq@open.ac.uk

The Open University
Walton Hall, Milton Keynes
MK7 6AA

First published 2007

Copyright © 2007 The Open University

All rights reserved. No part of this publication may be reproduced, stored in a retrieval system, transmitted or utilised in any form or by any means, electronic, mechanical, photocopying, recording or otherwise, without written permission from the publisher or a licence from the Copyright Licensing Agency Ltd. Details of such licences (for reprographic reproduction) may be obtained from the Copyright Licensing Agency Ltd of 90 Tottenham Court Road, London W1T 4LP.

Open University course materials may also be made available in electronic formats for use by students of the University. All rights, including copyright and related rights and database rights, in electronic course materials and their contents are owned by or licensed to The Open University, or otherwise used by The Open University as permitted by applicable law.

In using electronic course materials and their contents you agree that your use will be solely for the purposes of following an Open University course of study or otherwise as licensed by The Open University or its assigns.

Except as permitted above you undertake not to copy, store in any medium (including electronic storage or use in a website), distribute, transmit or retransmit, broadcast, modify or show in public such electronic materials in whole or in part without the prior written consent of The Open University or in accordance with the Copyright, Designs and Patents Act 1988.

Edited and designed by The Open University.

Typeset by The Open University

Printed in Great Britain by Bell & Bain Ltd., Glasgow

ISBN 978 0 7492 16870

1.1

B/a200_Block6_e1i1_N978074928877

The paper used in this publication contains pulp sourced from forests independently certified to the Forest Stewardship Council (FSC) principles and criteria. Chain of custody certification allows the pulp from these forests to be tracked to the end use (see www.fsc-uk.org).

CONTENTS

INTRODUCTION

Donna Loftus

WHAT YOU NEED TO STUDY THIS BLOCK

- Units 21–24
- *Course Guide*
- *Media Guide*
- *Visual Sources*
- Anthology documents
- Secondary sources
- DVD 3
- TMA 06

Learning outcomes

When you have finished this block you will have:

- learnt about European imperialism in the period 1870–1900, particularly in relation to Africa

- explored some of the debates about empire and the causes of imperialism, both at the time and among historians

- explored a number of key concepts in these debates, such as informal empire, new imperialism, jingoism, free trade, gentlemanly capitalism, social imperialism and genocide

- used case studies to consider in greater depth the impact of empire on the politics, economies and culture of the imperial powers

- widened your knowledge of the range of sources that historians use by looking at some sources that are particularly relevant to recent history, such as newspaper reports, business records, advertisements and publicity materials, and photographs

- conducted a simple search of an online database for evidence related to a historical enquiry

- learnt, using DVD 3, how imperialism has shaped public architecture and space in London and Brussels.

INTRODUCTION TO THE THEMES OF THE BLOCK

The expansion of western influence overseas had been taking place throughout the period covered in this course. However, in the late nineteenth century, imperialism appeared to be more aggressive and combative, bringing the European powers into greater conflict with each other and with those they were attempting to colonise. Similarly, while empire throughout the period covered in this course was associated with commerce and consumerism, and was driven by a demand for goods such as sugar, spices and textiles, by the 1890s a more aggressive form of capitalism appeared to be fuelling the more ruthless exploitation of the colonies, especially in Africa. This block asks you to consider whether, as some historians such as Niall Ferguson have argued, the expansion of three modern phenomena in the late nineteenth century – financial capitalism, the nation state and the mass media – pushed empire to the extremes that eventually resulted in the 'scramble' in which the European nations competed to colonise parts of Africa (Ferguson, 2004, p. 283).

The nations of Europe took different approaches to expansion overseas at different times: consider, for example, the differences between the British colonies of settlement, such as Canada and Australia, and the more aggressive forms of imperialism that Britain, France and Germany orchestrated in the so-called 'scramble for Africa'. This block concentrates on British, Belgian and German imperialism in the late nineteenth and early twentieth centuries. In particular, it will ask you to think about the relationship between empire and the nation, and the extent to which imperial expansion became associated with the 'modern' industrialised nations of Europe.

In recent years there has been a revival of interest in the history of empire. The subject was seen to be in decline in the 1970s in line with the process of formal decolonisation. The renewed interest in empire has been seen by some historians as having both personal and political roots. The increasing ethnic diversity of Britain and the popularity of family history have fuelled an awareness of connections with an imperial past. Meanwhile, geopolitical events, such as the extension of American foreign policy and the instability of some newly independent states, have led to an interest in the mechanisms of imperial rule. In many ways the reasons for the renewed interest have motivated different kinds of questions about the history of empire, and sometimes these new approaches sit uncomfortably with old ways of understanding the past (Marshall, 2003).

Traditional approaches to the history of empire have tended to focus on the motivation for expansion overseas and the nature of imperial domination. They have considered the extent to which imperial expansion was driven by increasingly competitive forms of industrial and financial capitalism, and pursued and sustained by nation states determined to ensure their share of the world's resources. More recent approaches have drawn on cultural history to consider how ideas about progress, civilisation and race were produced in sustaining imperial domination. Some studies have sought to recapture the experience of the colonised through histories of those 'subalterns' whose everyday life and culture was changed by imperial domination. Of greater concern in this block, however, are the studies of empire that consider the impact of imperialism on the metropole: the parent state of the colony. Historiography is, then, a key aspect of the block. All the units in this block will ask you to consider the different ways historians have approached the history of empire and the way contemporary concerns have influenced perspectives.

The block will show why the history of imperialism is important to any understanding of the European nation through a study of the so-called 'new imperialism' of the late nineteenth century. Unit 21 explores new imperialism and Britain – in particular through its relations with Africa. It will introduce some of the ways that ideas about Africa, imperialism and Britishness can be studied. Unit 22 explores a case study of Dundee to show the importance of economic history to understandings of empire. Unit 23 turns directly to the 'scramble for Africa' and, in particular, to the impact of King Leopold's pursuit of an empire in the Congo. Unit 24 takes up the history of German imperialism and considers how the aggressive nature of expansion in the period led to confrontations that became increasingly violent.

All of the course themes are relevant in this block. Unit 22 deals more directly with producers and consumers, but, as you will see, the issues of trade and resources are never far away from any discussion of empire. Similarly, all the units consider state formation, but the state is perceived as both the political institutions that make up the government and the 'nation' as it becomes defined through the process of overseas expansion. The theme of beliefs and ideologies is also central to all the units. Unit 21 deals most directly with the question of how ideas about empire are produced, circulated and debated, but all units in some way engage with the beliefs that helped support and sustain imperial expansion.

This block examines the interrelationship between the themes of the course by exploring some of the reasons for European imperialism and the impact of that expansion on the metropole. Although it is beyond the scope of this block, it is nevertheless important to recognise that European imperialism impacted on the nature of state formation, economic development and belief systems in countries that were once colonised by European nations. Lines were drawn, boundaries constructed, trade agreements sealed and ideas transported that have had a lasting legacy in these countries. The focus of this block is, however, on the relationship between European modernisation and imperialism in the late nineteenth and early twentieth centuries.

REFERENCES

Ferguson, N. (2004) *Empire. How Britain Made the Modern World*, London, Penguin.

Marshall, P.J. (2003) 'British imperial history "old" and "new"' in http://www.history.ac.uk/ihr/Focus/Empire/index.html.

Donna Loftus

INTRODUCTION

On Friday 18 May 1900, thousands of people took to the streets of London on hearing the news that British troops fighting in the Boer War in South Africa had relieved the small town of Mafeking, which Boer troops had kept under siege. Celebrations were echoed in towns and cities across Britain as the news was spread by the new half-penny daily press. 'Mafeking Night', as it became known, seemed to demonstrate the interest and enthusiasm that the average British citizen felt for the empire. The crowds on the streets, as captured in photographs and illustrations of the time, appeared to be genuinely popular, composed of a range of the people from across the class spectrum (see Figure 21.1 and *Visual Sources*, Plate 21.1). The story of how General Baden-Powell held out against the Boers for 217 days had been followed closely by the press, for it seemed to symbolise the characteristics of British imperialism: pluck, bravery and pride. News of relief appeared to unleash a spontaneous wave of patriotism for Britain and the empire, and admiration for the heroes, such as Baden-Powell, who embodied the nation's pride.

The events of the 18 May seemed to show Britain at the highpoint of imperial endeavour. More than ever, British popular culture appeared to be steeped in imperialism: adventure stories, the daily reports of the popular press, exhibitions and spectacles, such as the Greater Britain Exhibition of 1899, and national celebrations, such as Queen Victoria's jubilee celebrations of 1897, presented Britain as an imperial nation, its beneficial influence spreading across the globe. At the same time, the war in South Africa (1899–1902) appeared to represent all that was wrong with the British empire. As critics of empire, such as J. A. Hobson, pointed out, its administration was expensive and its defence took precious lives while the benefits appeared to go to a few with investments and trade interests in the colonised regions. As one historian of the British empire, P. J. Marshall, has argued, the war was 'an imperial crisis of gigantic proportions' that exposed all the faults and tensions of empire (Marshall, 1996, p. 64). The siege of Mafeking could also be seen as demonstrating Britain's diplomatic isolation and the difficulty the British army had defeating the Boers.

This unit will ask you to think about the nature of British imperialism in the late nineteenth century. You will consider questions about the motivations for imperial expansion and the way imperialism was understood at home. This will link with the themes of the course in a number of ways. You will have to think about state formation: what role did government play in imperial expansion? Producers and consumers will be considered through a brief discussion of the economic motivations behind imperialism, and the theme of beliefs and

Figure 21.1   A. and G. Taylor, Relief of Mafeking: celebrating crowds throng the streets of London, 18 May 1900, photograph. Photo: Mary Evans Picture Library

ideologies will be taken up in aspects of the unit that consider how ideas about empire were produced and understood. The unit will get you to think about the links between the three themes through a consideration of the relationship between the state, economics and culture. To address these questions thoroughly you would have to move between a history of Britain and the histories of its colonised territories. The approach taken in this unit is essentially British centred in that it seeks to study how events overseas were understood in Britain. In so doing, the unit will begin to consider how important the empire was to Britain in the late nineteenth century.

The unit will ask you to consider these questions in relation to British imperialism in Africa because Africa, along with south-east Asia, was the primary focus of new British imperial activity in the late nineteenth century. The conquest of Africa at that time is associated with the aggressive and competitive form of colonisation that has become known as 'new imperialism'.

EXERCISE

Before you begin, I want you to get a sense of the extent of the British empire. Look at the map in the *Visual Sources*, Plate 21.2.

What impression does this give you of the British empire at the end of the nineteenth century?

Spend about 5 minutes on this exercise.

DISCUSSION

As the note in the bottom left-hand corner states, this is a map of 'The World' on which 'The British possessions are coloured red'. The British empire appears to cover a quite considerable area: it stretches from the West Indies to India and includes colonies of settlement in Canada, Australia and South Africa, as well as parts of Africa and many islands scattered throughout the globe. The red colouring given to British territories created a pictorial image of an empire that was tangible and coherent with Great Britain at its centre.

DISCUSSION

Great Britain was often presented in nineteenth-century world maps as the centre of a vast coherent empire but, during the century, its relationships with its 'possessions' was complex, shifting and largely framed by the way that each territory had been acquired and the constituency of the population. For a start, contemporaries distinguished colonies of settlement, such as Canada, Australia and South Africa, to which many Europeans had migrated and set up home, from territories such as India and Africa, in which Europeans tended not to settle (apart from the manpower associated with colonial administration and defence, some traders and missionaries). The former countries were free to develop their own forms of representative government in the nineteenth century, while British colonial administrators preferred to keep closer control of the latter, albeit sometimes with the acquiescence of local rulers. As the historian Bernard Porter said of the British empire in the mid nineteenth century 'There was no single language covering the whole empire, no one religion, no one code of law'. In fact, Porter went as far as to say that in the mid nineteenth century there was 'no kind of overall logic' governing the British empire (Porter, 1996, p. 7).

The very absence of coherence and centralised control in the expansion of British influence overseas during the eighteenth century and early nineteenth century led J. R. Seeley, chair of modern history at Cambridge, to argue in his influential book *The Expansion of England* that Britain acquired an empire in a fit of absence of mind. Published in 1883, Seeley's book represented a renewed interest in the British empire in the late nineteenth century which called for more direct state interest in colonies, a so-called Greater Britain (Seeley, 1883, pp. 8, 11). Seeley used 'colonies' to mean colonies of settlement; for him the 'colonial empire' was the 'white empire'. His lectures were an argument for what was later called 'imperial federation' – the idea that there should be closer working arrangements between the dominions and Britain, such as an imperial parliament.

This sort of interest in the question of imperialism was one of the factors that made the expansion of the late nineteenth century seem different. Eric Hobsbawn, one of Britain's leading historians, made this observation about the term 'imperialism':

> In short, it was a novel term used to describe a novel phenomenon. This evident fact is enough to dismiss one of the many schools in the tense and highly charged ideological debate about 'imperialism', namely the one which argues that it was nothing new, perhaps even that it was a mere pre-capitalist survival. It was, at any rate, felt to be new and was discussed as a novelty.
>
> (Hobsbawn, 1997, p. 60)

Why was the imperialism of the late nineteenth century felt to be new? Is there any evidence that imperialism in this period involved new kinds of expansion?

NEW IMPERIALISM AND THE LATE NINETEENTH-CENTURY NATION: AFRICA AND THE VICTORIANS

Until late in the nineteenth century, Britain's interests in Africa were mostly limited to the Cape Colony in the south, West African coastal areas, such as Sierra Leone and The Gambia, a network of forts on the Gold Coast (Ghana) with some trading links, such as those on the Niger river, pushing British interests inland (see Figures 21.2 and 21.3). Yet by 1900 Britain had acquired formal colonies in East, Central and West Africa and had also occupied Egypt and Sudan (Marshall, 1996, p. 72) (see Figure 21.4). The map of Africa in the *Visual Sources*, Plate 21.3, shows how the continent was represented in an atlas of 1912.

The idea that there was something new and different about late nineteenth-century imperialism appears to result from two related phenomena. The first is the intensification of intervention overseas, which brought the British government into conflict with those it sought to colonise and with other European nations, particularly in Africa. The second is the increasingly popular awareness of this at home, reflected in heightened interest in the

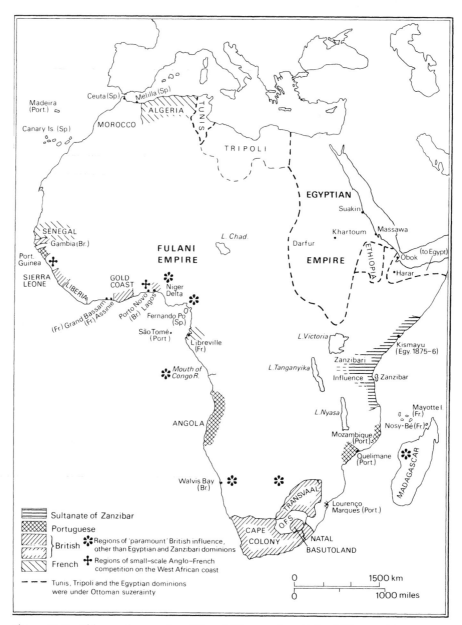

Figure 21.2 Africa on the eve of partition, 1878, map from Roland Oliver and G. N. Sanderson (eds) *The Cambridge History of Africa*, vol. 6, Cambridge, Cambridge University Press, 1997, p. 118

question of imperialism. The rate of territorial expansion was almost as great in earlier decades of the nineteenth century, but the debate that surrounded the later expansion was greater. According to Marshall 'What was strikingly new about the later nineteenth century was the intensity of public debate about empire' (Marshall, 1996, p. 54).

Throughout the nineteenth century, a vast range of attitudes to empire can be identified with no one view achieving total hegemony, although at certain

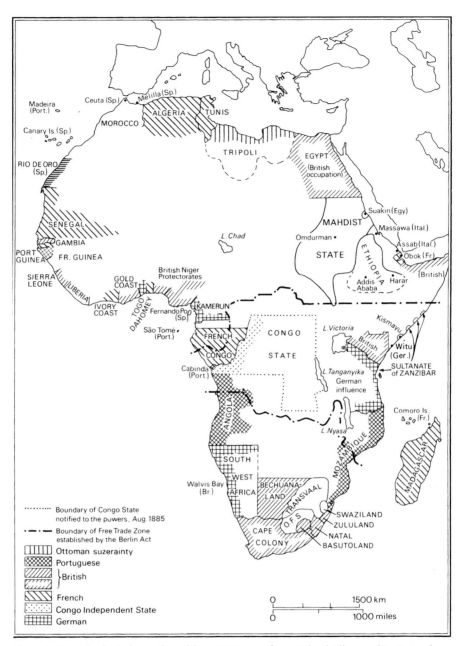

Figure 21.3   The first phase of partition, 1887, map from Roland Oliver and G. N. Sanderson (eds) *The Cambridge History of Africa*, vol. 6, Cambridge, Cambridge University Press, 1997, p. 140

moments distinct arguments gained precedence. In the first half of the century, some politicians and political economists were highly critical of the British empire and its administration, believing it to be expensive and unnecessary. Instead, advocates of free-trade liberalism promoted a view of the British empire as a conglomerate of free-trading, self-governing colonies. The Colonial Society was one such organisation; it was formed in the mid

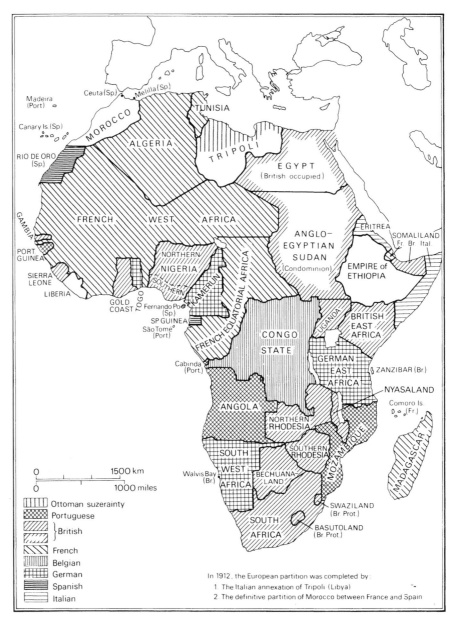

Figure 21.4   Africa partitioned, 1902, from Roland Oliver and G. N. Sanderson (eds) *The Cambridge History of Africa*, vol. 6, Cambridge, Cambridge University Press, 1997, p. 152

nineteenth century by liberal politicians and economists such as John Bright and Richard Cobden to campaign for self-government for the colonies. The Colonial Society combined paternalistic and democratic arguments in its vision of the empire. It saw the colonies as needing the protection and guidance of the mother country, until, like the children of a well-organised family, they were able to maintain themselves in a universal brotherhood of free-trading partners. Its view influenced other liberal thinkers such John Stuart Mill, who believed that colonial subjects were capable of freedom once educated and civilised by enlightened British colonisers.

This hegemony of liberalism and free trade did not necessarily translate into a lack of interest in empire. Throughout the nineteenth century, alongside the formal annexation of territory, Britain extended its influence overseas through a network of trading links that have become known as 'informal empire' (you will consider this in more detail in Unit 22). In this system of 'informal empire', British sea-power 'safe-guarded and even created the conditions of free trade which guaranteed Britain's economic preponderance', a system of imperialism that was, on the whole, deemed to be preferable to the trouble and expense of formal annexation (Sanderson, 1997a, p. 97).

In the 1850s, 1860s and 1870s, unrest and outright opposition to British authority in some parts of the colonies severely tested the paternal imagery of them as emerging into independent nationhood, and the protectionist policies of other nations challenged the notion of a universal free-trading brotherhood. As Catherine Hall has argued, after rebellions in the colonies, such as the Indian rebellion of 1857 and the Jamaica uprising of 1865, the liberal colonialism of men like Cobden and Mill began to give way to the view of men like Thomas Carlyle and Charles Dilke that the white races were superior and destined always to dominate over others – a belief that demanded the government aggressively defend British imperial interests (Hall, 1992, p. 255). At the same time, Britain's informal control came under increased threat from other European nations whose attempts to gain an empire required them to thwart British competition through more formal possessions (Sanderson, 1997a, p. 101). Increasingly, the writers on empire that gained public prominence placed ideas of the nation at the heart of imperial endeavour. Seeley's arguments called for greater coherence in imperial policy: he argued that the dominance of free-trade thought in the early nineteenth century led to a lack of interest in the formal recognition of empire. Without a more coherent and unified imperial organisation, Seeley argued, Britain and the British empire would stagnate and decline, leaving it unable to face growing competition from other European powers. His arguments persuaded many in the context of the recent depression of trade that had occurred in Britain in the 1870s and 1880s (Sanderson, 1997a, p. 96).

> To what extent, then, was the imperialism in Africa of the late nineteenth century motivated by economic concerns and trade interests, and further fuelled by European competition?

The big question!

This is quite a difficult question to answer because Britain's 'interests' in Africa in the late nineteenth century were orchestrated in a piecemeal fashion through a variety of individuals, agencies and institutions. Throughout the nineteenth century, Christian missions were very much involved in bringing what many saw as the benefits of civilisation to Africa by building churches and schools. Explorers such as David Livingstone and Henry Morton Stanley undertook to uncover lands unknown to the British people and sent eagerly anticipated reports home that were popularised in the press. Many such reports saw Africa as an 'El Dorado' of resources and markets that would stimulate the industrial economy (Sanderson, 1997a, pp. 96–102). But, such sentiments did not necessarily lead to a change in colonial policy. Many businessmen had their own interests and traded with African states for raw materials such as palm oil with little interference from the British government.

On the whole, when the British government did lay claim to a territory, usually to secure trade from the incursion of other European powers and the perceived whims of African leaders, it did so by using private bodies rather than direct control. Thus the British government awarded charters – documents that conferred rights on a group or company – to allow private companies to govern territory. In this way, the British government contracted out its interests in Africa. For example, the Royal Niger Company was chartered in 1886 to take care of British claims on the Niger. The Imperial British East Africa Company was formed in 1888 to run territory in East Africa ceded by Germany to Britain in 1886 and, perhaps most well known, The British South Africa Company (BSAC) was chartered in 1889 to occupy part of Zimbabwe that became known as Rhodesia. These chartered companies were given exclusive economic rights to mineral resources and could compel Africans to labour and pay taxes; the BSAC gained title to vast areas of land. Despite this pattern of intervention, events in Egypt and South Africa brought the British government into direct conflict in Africa and appeared to show the British government exercising direct control to protect economic interests.

EXERCISE

British intervention in Egypt and South Africa is key to arguments about the new, more aggressive type of imperialism in the late nineteenth century. Read these brief histories of Egypt, Sudan and South Africa. After you have read them, you will be asked to consider the reasons why the British government decided to intervene in each territory.

Egypt

Egypt was part of the Ottoman empire ruled by the sultan in Constantinople. Through the 1870s, European banks had invested large quantities of money in Egypt and made many loans to Prince Ismail Pasha (Khedive Ismāil). In 1875, increasingly unable to keep his creditors at bay, the khedive sold his shares in the recently built Suez Canal. The British Conservative prime minister, Disraeli, aware that control of the Suez was crucial in protecting Britain's route to India, bought the shares and with them 44 per cent of the capital of the Suez Canal Company. But Egyptian foreign debt continued to soar and by 1876 it was bankrupt. Many countries, Britain and France in particular, were owed considerable sums of money. In 1879, Ismail was deposed and Britain and France effectively took dual control of the management of Egypt's finances. In the meantime, a rebellion was growing, led by Ahmed Bey Arabi (Urābī) a colonel in the Egyptian army who expressed a popular dissatisfaction with corruption among the Turkish upper class and interference from foreign powers in Egypt. Gladstone, who had replaced Disraeli in 1880, had a reputation as an anti-imperial Liberal prime minister but reluctantly agreed to restore order, as exaggerated reports reached London of rioting in the port of Alexandria in which Christians were being massacred. In July 1882, making full use of military technology, the British bombarded the port of Alexandria and invaded Egypt with brutal efficiency (see Figure 21.5). Arabi's forces were soon defeated at Tell-el-Kebir. Evelyn Baring, first earl of Cromer, a member of the famous banking

Figure 21.5 Photographer Unknown, Alexandria after the British bombardment, July 1882. Photo: Corbis Images

family and part of the Indian administration, was given the title British Agent and Consul-General (Sanderson, 1997b, pp. 606–8). The British did not annex Egypt but administered the country through an Egyptian government. This arrangement raised tensions between the British and French, the latter making frequent requests to know when the British would implement their intention to leave Egypt (Mitchell, 1988, pp. 128–30).

Initially, British policy makers did not see Egypt as an imperial possession. In the late 1880s, policy appears to have changed: Britain decided to remain. In 1883, there were 170 British officials in Egypt, by 1906 there were 662 (Marshall, 1996, p. 74). Also, Egypt had an empire of sorts itself and Britain was subsequently drawn into further action to defend Egypt, action that would severely test Anglo-French relations (Waites, 1999, p. 124).

Sudan

While British civil servants took control of the administration of Egypt, a force of resistance was emerging in Sudan, a vast territory over which Egypt had influence. Egyptian armies under Mehemet Ali had conquered the territory in the 1830s. In 1881, Muhammad Ahmad ibn 'Abdallāh, claiming to be the Mahdi (the Guided One of the Prophet), began a campaign against Egyptian rule in a bid to create an Islamic community (Sanderson, 1997b, p. 609). By the time the British established their presence in Egypt, the Mahdi had raised a considerable army and taken control of Sudan from the Egyptian forces. The British government argued that they were not responsible for Sudan, but did send a force led by General Gordon to try to get the Egyptian forces out of Sudan. Gordon arrived in Khartoum in February 1884, but instead of evacuating troops he demanded a British expedition to 'smash up the Mahdi' (Sanderson, 1997b, p. 616). He was subsequently cornered by Mahdi forces. Gladstone's government, irritated by Gordon's refusal to follow orders to leave Khartoum, at first refused to intervene but eventually gave in to public pressure and sent a force out from Cairo in September. In January 1885, the Mahdi, gaining news of the imminent arrival of the relieving army, ordered an attack on Khartoum in which Gordon was killed, supposedly on the stairs of his palace (see *Visual Sources*, Plate 21.4). In England, angry crowds blamed Gladstone for Gordon's death.

The myths and legends that were subsequently constructed around Gordon helped to keep Sudan in the public consciousness. At various times calls were made for the reconquest of Sudan, referring to the brutality of the Sudanese regime, the continuation of the slave trade there and the need to secure Egypt and protect the Nile. The conflict was seen by some as having religious overtones; some argued that the Mahdi was intent on a holy war against Britain (Robinson and Gallagher, 1981, p. 157). In 1895, the Liberal government gave way to the more imperialistic Conservatives led by Salisbury and, soon after, a joint British and Egyptian campaign for the reconquest of Sudan began under the leadership of General Kitchener. Kitchener's army, with its superior military technology, slaughtered the Mahdists in their thousands at Omdurman in 1898 (see Figures 21.6 and 21.7, and Plate 21.5). It then proceeded to take Khartoum (Sanderson, 1997b, p. 640). At the same time, a French mission under the leadership of Captain Jean-Baptiste Marchand went out to challenge British influence in staking a claim to the Nile basin, an area considered important to Egypt's security and prosperity. The two groups met at Fashoda. The respective newspapers of both countries attacked each other with virulence, both claiming Sudan was theirs to occupy (Sanderson, 1997, p. 150). The crisis abated

THE BATTLE OF OMDURMAN: THE 11TH SOUDANESE IN THE TRENCHES AWAITING THE DERVISH ATTACK

Figure 21.6 Battle of Omdurman showing the 11th Sudanese in the trenches awaiting the Dervish attack, 2 September 1898, printed from a photograph by Captain E.A. Stanton. Photo: Mary Evans Picture Library. 'Dervish' means a member of a muslim fraternity vowed to poverty. However, the term was used pejoratively by British commentators to refer to Sudanese supporters of the Mahdi in the 1890s

THE BATTLE OF OMDURMAN: MAXIMS READY TO FIRE ON THE ADVANCING DERVISHES

From a Photograph by Captain E. A. Stanton

Figure 21.7 Battle of Omdurman showing maxims ready to fire on the advancing Dervishes, 2 September 1898, printed from a photograph by Captain E.A. Stanton. Photo: Mary Evans Picture Library

when the French withdrew their claims. Kitchener returned to Britain – his hero's welcome soon becoming an anti-French demonstration. Kitchener went on to become the first governor-general of Anglo-Egyptian Sudan.

Charles George Gordon (1833–85), a deeply committed Christian, was an army officer. In 1855, he went out to serve in the Crimean War (1853–56) and in 1858 he joined forces in the Second Opium War, or Arrow War (1856–60). Gordon made his name as the commander of a force that successfully defended the city of Shanghai in 1863 from the Taiping uprising, a revolt against the Qing empire in China. He returned to England in 1865 as a popular hero, known in the press as 'Chinese Gordon'. He was appointed governor of Equatoria in Sudan 1873, and governor-general in 1876. Gordon worked to eradicate the slave trade until ill health forced him to return to England in 1880. In January 1884, he agreed to a request from King Leopold II of Belgium to act for him in the Congo; however, at the same time a press campaign orchestrated by W. T. Stead of the *Pall Mall Gazette* demanded that Gordon return to Sudan to save British and Egyptian forces from the Mahdi. Despite questions about Gordon's reliability, in February 1884 the British government sent Gordon to evacuate Egyptian forces and civilians trapped by the Mahdi's forces in Khartoum. Gordon was subsequently besieged at Khartoum for 317 days. The Mahdi's forces entered Khartoum on 26 January 1885 and killed Gordon along with other soldiers and civilians in the city. His body was never found. Gordon was known by those who had worked with him for his impulsiveness and poor judgement; nevertheless, the public blamed Gladstone for Gordon's death because of his failure to act swiftly in sending a relieving force to Khartoum.

The South African War

In the same period, British interests in South Africa were also causing conflicts in Africa and raising tensions in Europe. In the first half of the nineteenth century, South Africa was not considered economically important. The Cape of Good Hope was annexed in 1806 more because it provided a strategically important port on the route to India. The Cape population included the indigenous peoples, the Khoikhoi, and the Afrikaners, a group numbering about 30,000 descended from Dutch settlers, mostly scattered as farmers (or 'Boers'). Between 1836 and 1846, about 14,000 Afrikaners undertook the 'Great Trek' north to avoid British rule, a move that brought them into conflict with the African peoples who lived in these lands (Marshall, 1996, p. 40). The Orange Free State and the South African Republic (Transvaal) were established as Afrikaner republics and for a while the British left these areas alone.

In the second half of the nineteenth century, tensions were raised by the establishment of a German presence on the coast of South-West Africa, fuelling fears of a German–Afrikaner alliance against Britain, and by the discovery of gold in the Rand of the Transvaal at Witwatersrand (Marshall, 1996, p. 135). This discovery of gold, together with the existing diamond mines, made the South African Republic central to the world money market (Marks, 1997, p. 424). A flood of developers and companies poured into the region. These were known as uitlanders, or outsiders, to the Afrikaner Boer population. The Boer president, Paul Kruger, refused to grant these newcomers civil rights while taxing them heavily for their exploitation of his land. One of these companies from outside the Transvaal involved in mining for gold was the Consolidated Gold Fields of Cecil Rhodes.

Cecil Rhodes was the multimillionaire owner of diamond mines at Kimberley and prime minister of the Cape from 1890 to 1896. He obtained a royal charter in 1889 for his British South Africa Company. He soon acquired a stretch of land, as yet unclaimed by European powers, to which he gave his name: Rhodesia. This land was won at a price: although it gave Rhodes access to massive profits, it brought him into frequent conflict with the local Ndebele people. Despite this, he harboured further desires to expand British interests in the region and, in particular, to build a Cape to Cairo railway link – a plan that could not be realised without the cooperation or conquest of the Boer republics (see the cartoon 'The Rhodes Colossus' from *Punch* 10 December 1892 in the Anthology, p. 401). Tensions between the Boers and the British presence in the Cape over resources and land were further exacerbated by the events of 1895 that have become known as the Jameson Raid. In December 1895, Rhodes, together with one of his closest associates, Dr Leander Starr Jameson, decided to exploit uitlander unhappiness and encouraged a revolt against the Boers which Rhodes would support with his own private army and use to establish a British Transvaal. Despite the covert support of Chamberlain, colonial secretary in Salisbury's Conservative government, the plot misfired. No rising took place but Jameson had already sent in his army, which was defeated. There was an outcry in Britain that was, to some extent, eclipsed by anti-German sentiment roused when the German Kaiser sent a telegram to Kruger congratulating him on his success against the British.

The British government, determined not to lose face, maintained the pressure on Kruger's government to give rights to the uitlanders. Chamberlain presented the issue as a test of Britain's power and authority in the wider world. Negotiations broke down and war broke out. It lasted from 1899 to 1902, involved nearly 400,000 imperial troops and cost £250 million (Marshall, 1996, p. 66). Initially, support for the war was strong and British confidence in its military and technological superiority was high, but after some spectacular early defeats and vigorous guerrilla resistance, the British took to destroying Boer farms and took women and children into concentration camps. Around 28,000 white inmates died in such camps, most of them children. Africans were also herded into labour camps in attempts to clear rural areas. Mortality figures are sketchy but by 1901 official figures claimed that 13,315 Africans died, although the real figure is probably much higher (Marks, 1997, p. 479). Britain had little support in Europe – its actions were seen as murder and plunder – and public opinion in Britain began to turn against the war (see Figures 21.8 and 21.9 and Plate 21.8).

Are there any similarities in the history of British intervention in Egypt, Sudan and South Africa? Think of some very general points.

Spend about 15 minutes on this exercise.

LES CAMPS DE RECONCENTRATION

..... Grâce à la bonne organisation des camps de reconcentration l'abondance et la santé y règnent. C'est un véritable plaisir de voir les enfants courir et jouer innocemment entre les tentes sous l'œil souriant de leurs mères qui oublient ainsi un moment la mélancolie de leur position.....

..... Les mesures de précaution que nous avons prises ont abaissé la mortalité des enfants à 380 pour mille.

(Rapport officiel au War Office.)

414

Figure 21.8   Jean Veber, 'Les camps de reconcentration', caricature of the Boer War, from *L'Assiette au Beurre*, 28 September 1901. Photo: © Private Collection / Archives Charmet / The Bridgeman Art Library. The caption reads: 'The concentration camps. Thanks to the good organisation of the concentration camps, health and plenty are prevalent. It is a real pleasure to watch children running and playing innocently between the tents under the happy smiles of their mothers, who can forget for a moment their sad situation …
The preventative measures we have taken have reduced the child mortality rate to 380 per 1000.'

Figure 21.9   Jean Veber, 'Galanterie Britannique', or 'British Gallantry', a French criticism of the evils of a British concentration camp for Boer women and children. Photo: © Private Collection / Topham Picturepoint / The Bridgeman Art Library. The caption reads: 'British gallantry. I have to acknowledge the proverbial gallantry of the British soldier and pay him homage. Each day many examples are brought to my attention. It is touching to see with what regard, what care, the Boer women are treated.'

Cecil John Rhodes (1853–1902) was a businessman, colonial politician and imperialist. He was born in Bishop Stortford, Herts. His father, Francis William Rhodes, was the local vicar. He joined his brother as a cotton farmer in Natal in South Africa in the 1870s, but in 1871 joined the mass of people who travelled to Kimberley after the discovery of diamonds in the area. Rhodes quickly accumulated a lot of money through diamond mining. In 1880, he founded the DeBeer's Mining Company with Charles Rudd, which soon had control of most of the Kimberley mines. In 1880, he entered politics, becoming the representative for Barkly West in the Cape parliament and prime minister of the Cape Colony in 1890. He used his power to promote mining interests. In 1886, Rhodes became convinced that there was gold to be found in the area between the Limpopo and Zambesi rivers, territory ruled by King Lobengula and populated by the Ndebele (Matabele) people. In a bid to beat other powers to the gold, Rhodes and Rudd persuaded Lobengula to sign a treaty giving Rhodes mining rights in the area. In 1889, the British government gave Rhodes's British South Africa Company a charter to exercise control of a region north of British Bechuanaland that included land used by the Ndebele (Matabeleland) and the Shona tribes (Mashonaland). The subsequent incursion of white settlers increased friction and led to wars with the Ndebele and Shona people of Matabeleland and Mashonaland between 1893 and 1897. With victory, the BSAC took control of the territory belonging to the Ndebele and Shona that became known as Southern Rhodesia (later Zimbabwe). The BSAC went on to take land north of the Zambesi, which became known as Northern Rhodesia (later Zambia). His desire to open up central Africa to British commercial interests resulted in the disastrous Jameson raid of 1895, an event that forced his resignation as prime minister of the Cape Colony. Rhodes died in the Cape in 1902.

SPECIMEN ANSWER

Clearly British intervention in Egypt, Sudan and South Africa had specific causes; however, in very general terms, resources and ensuring security in the context of regional instability and European rivalry appear to be factors influencing officials. In the 1880s, the instability of the regime in Egypt was a matter of some concern for those Europeans who had invested in the country. Intervention in Sudan may have been part of a strategy to further protect these interests by ensuring the security of the Nile. In South Africa, the discovery of gold raised tensions in the region, as did Rhodes's perceived need to protect his investments and promote his desire to build railways in the region.

DISCUSSION

The economic motivations to intervention appear to be clear: in both Egypt and South Africa instability and European rivalry eroded the conditions that enabled informal empire to exist. But other issues also need explanation. According to Cromer, the British consul-general in Egypt, southern Sudan included 'large tracts of useless territory which it would be difficult and costly to administer properly' and northern Sudan would take a lot of investment to make it profitable (quoted in Sanderson, 1997a, p. 151). Nevertheless, the protection of Britain's influence in Egypt and Sudan was also seen as a test of its power and a symbol of its influence, issues that appeared to rouse public interest, especially with respect to the death of Gordon and the Fashoda incident. British military superiority enabled it to occupy

Egypt with ruthless force and, despite the slaughter of thousands of Mahdists, a protracted conflict was nevertheless avoided. The escalation of tension in South Africa was less easily resolved and ultimately led to a war that shattered British confidence.

Intervention seems, then, to be a result of a combination of factors: economic concerns, security, national pride and the technological superiority that made it possible. The relationship between these factors requires further investigation.

CRITICS OF IMPERIALISM

J. A. Hobson argued that empire exploited the British public and the colonised to make a lot of money for the few. His work has strongly influenced the historiography on empire. The notion that there was something new and distinct about late nineteenth-century imperialism stems in part from the criticisms that contemporaries such as Hobson produced. Hobson's writing on imperialism suggested a clear link between the export of capital (investment overseas) and the drive to annex the territory where such investments were made. Although he was unable to prove a causal link (that imperialism was directly motivated or 'caused' by the desire to protect and promote investments overseas), the writings of Hobson were significant in arguing that economics were the 'taproot' of imperialism.

> **John A. Hobson** (1858–1940) was a British radical liberal economist. His interest in imperialism was rooted in a wider concern with the social and economic problems that he, and many of his contemporaries, identified in late nineteenth-century Britain, such as poverty and unemployment. Some imperialists, such as Seeley and Chamberlain, argued that a more formal and controlled British empire would increase the prosperity of Britain through increased trade. Hobson employed a very different kind of reasoning. Like many free-trade liberals, he was disturbed by the high costs and brutality associated with colonial expansion and he began to see a clear link between the surplus capital acquired through the unequal distribution of wealth in Britain and expansion overseas. His experience as a journalist in South Africa during the Boer War persuaded him that imperialism was caused by aggressive capitalism. He developed his theory of the link between capitalism and imperialism further in *Imperialism: A Study* (Hobson, 1988 [1902]). Hobson was not necessarily anti-imperialist – he thought imperialism based on democracy and free trade would bring peace and prosperity to many nations (Cain, 2002).

EXERCISE

Read Anthology Document 6.1, 'Theories of imperialism', which is an extract from Hobson's *Imperialism: A Study*. As you will see, this extract is divided into three sections. Try to summarise the argument of each section in one or two sentences and then use these sentences to answer the question below and the question in the next exercise. This will help you deconstruct Hobson's argument and understand its significance. Think, in particular, about the emphasis that Hobson gives to political, economic and cultural factors in the motivation for imperial expansion.

What, according to Hobson, is new about the imperialism of the late nineteenth century?

Spend about 5 minutes on this exercise.

SPECIMEN ANSWER   The new imperialism emerges out of new forms of nationalism that are more competitive. Combined with the conditions of modern capitalism, this new nationalism leads nations into a 'fight for markets'. The new imperialism involves tighter, more direct control of territories by the British government. It is primarily motivated by the economic conditions of the time, in which manufacturing industry produces more than the population can consume and profitable uses for surplus capital cannot be found. As a result, businessmen look overseas for future opportunities.

EXERCISE   What about other motivations to imperialism that the unit has covered, such as the civilising mission – the desire to spread Christianity? Does Hobson recognise these forces?

Spend about 5 minutes on this exercise.

SPECIMEN ANSWER   Hobson is clearly unconvinced by the combining of business and benevolent motives in empire. Instead, at the end of the passage he suggests that an alliance of business and politics enabled Cecil Rhodes to manipulate the events and ideas to further his desire to push British influence in South Africa further north.

DISCUSSION   Hobson recognised the importance of ideas or, as he calls it, 'the imaginative' to imperialism, but he saw these as second to more selfish financial concerns. As he said:

> Imperialist politicians, soldiers, or company directors, who push forward policy by portraying the cruelties of the African slave raids ... or who open out a new field for missionary enterprise in China or the Soudan, do not deliberately or consciously work up these motives in order to incite British public. They simply and instinctively attach to themselves any strong, genuine elevated feeling which is of service, fan it and feed it until it assumes fervour, and utilize it for their ends.
>
> (Hobson, 1988 [1902], p. 197)

He also recognised that the political environment of the period, what he called competitive nationalisms, heightened tensions. Ultimately, for Hobson, economics was the 'taproot' of imperialism.

In response to Hobson's theory and its consideration by Lenin in 1915–16 (see Anthology Document 6.2, 'Imperialism and capitalism'), many historians have questioned the extent to which the new imperialism was motivated by economics by looking at the benefits of empire compared with its costs – you will take up some of these arguments in Unit 22. One of the strongest rebuttals of the association between new imperialism and new competitive forms of capitalism emerged in 1953 from the historians Robinson and Gallagher (Gallagher and Robinson, 1953). In their subsequent detailed study of imperialism in Africa Gallagher and Robinson could find no evidence of new motivations to expansion among businessmen and politicians. Instead, they argue that the history of expansion shows that there was no strategic alliance of politics and business. In particular, they point to official interest in East Africa and the Nile Valley despite the better potential for markets and raw materials in West Africa to argue that 'These regions of Africa which interested the British investor and merchant least, concerned ministers the most' (Robinson and Gallagher, 1981, p. 462). They pointed out that there was a motivation to 'integrate newly colonized regions and ancient agrarian empires into the industrial economy as markets and investments' and a 'strategic imperative to secure them against rivals in world power politics'. But, they argued, this did not necessitate empire: 'If they had done, the territorial scrambles of the late nineteenth century would have taken place in the Americas, where Europe was exporting the bulk of its economic and human resources, rather than in Africa and Asia' (p. 485).

It is, however, difficult not to prioritise economic motivations when considering the case of South Africa, not least because of the discovery of gold at a time that many countries had adopted the Gold Standard – a currency system that required the securing of precious metal supplies. The question is whether the specific conditions that informed British imperialism in South Africa can be generalised into a theory of imperialism that is then applied to expansion across the globe. This emphasis on the local particularity of British imperialism in Africa has informed recent studies that have questioned the way theories of imperialism have dominated the historiography of imperialism. In particular, Andrew Porter has argued that the South African War was a specific response to a very particular set of circumstances rather than an event that represented a 'new' kind of imperialism in the late nineteenth century and criticises historians for stretching the facts of the war to fit theories of imperialism.

EXERCISE

Find Andrew Porter's article 'The South African War (1899–1902): context and motive reconsidered' in the secondary sources on the course website. Read it now. In it, Porter engages with debates about the causes of the South African War. His article is useful for the summaries it provides of the existing historiography, but this also makes it quite difficult to read. What do you think is the significance of Porter's approach to the South African War? This is a complex issue, so I will move straight to a discussion rather than providing a specimen answer.

Spend about 2 hours on this exercise.

DISCUSSION

In the first three parts, Porter considers the historiography of the war and questions the way historians have used contexts to shore up their arguments that economics was the primary motivation for British intervention. The example he gives is of the 'context' of the rise of finance capital in London, so-called gentlemanly capitalism, in which business and politics merged to secure investments overseas (you will deal with this more thoroughly in Unit 22). Porter accepts that some capitalists gained from the war but argues that you cannot use this as evidence of a causative 'relationship' (i.e. that economics was the root of the war). Porter claims that the economic context of the new imperialism may simply be coinciding events that are not necessarily related.

In sections IV and V, Porter puts forward his argument that any understanding of imperialism needs to consider the context of metropolitan politics. You should note that Porter does not mean a 'liberal individualist' approach focusing on intentions of individual politicians but, instead, the influence of political institutions and political culture. In particular, he considers the actions and ambitions of men like Chamberlain and Milner as significant. Also important in attracting support for the war was Chamberlain's ability to associate the conflict with concerns about morality, justice and political reform – issues that were of great concerns in Britain at the time.

Porter's argument is significant in its dismissal of the idea that there is a 'new' economic motive to imperialism demonstrated in the causes of the South African War. Instead he sees the 'traditional' desire to ensure the security of Britain's existing interests as the key factor in persuading the government to go to war. Chamberlain and Milner played an important role in the context of political culture and institutions at home, especially the 'recently created democratic system'. Porter argues that Chamberlain was able to accommodate intervention overseas to domestic interests by linking the South African cause to questions of justice and morality (the civil rights of the uitlanders). As such, war was motivated by the traditional concern with security and it was enabled through the political strategy of men like Chamberlain and Milner, and not through the political dominance of their imperial vision or through the production of a 'larger vision of economic imperialism promoted by calculated aggression'.

Recap

With reference to the work of Hobson, many historians have argued that the examples of Egypt and South Africa demonstrate that new imperialism was a more aggressive form of intervention motivated through an alliance of financial capital and the state which dragged the government into conflict to protect British claims to profit-making resources in the region. Whether or not there is enough evidence to support this depends on extent to which historians focus on the particularities of intervention in different parts of Africa or on the common factors.

According to Porter, there is little evidence to support the notion of a new strategy of imperialism motivated by economics, backed by the state's foreign policy and carried out through confrontation and aggression. He argues that the work of Hobson and Lenin should be seen as contemporary responses to particular events rather than theories of new imperialism. Whether the evidence is there to support the case for a new imperialism or not, it is clear in the responses of men like Hobson that some people felt they were living in a new imperial age (a point that Hobsbawn made earlier in this unit). Also, although the work of Robinson and Gallagher refers to the particular reasons

only because of the public's perception of "empire"

for intervention in different parts of Africa, some general questions still need answering. As Robinson and Gallagher themselves acknowledge, there is still a need to explain how a 'handful of European pro-consuls managed to manipulate the polymorphic societies of Africa and Asia' (Robinson and Gallagher, 1981, p. 485). Related to this is the question of how a minority of imperialists like Chamberlain managed to persuade the British public and the British government to support or, at the very least, not to protest about their imperial interests.

In addressing this question, the rest of the unit will change focus to look at how ideas about empire were produced. It deals with the theme of beliefs and ideologies most directly but, as you work through these sections, consider the way all three themes interrelate. You will need to think about the way that commerce, politics and culture interact in ideas of empire and whether, for example, the British public was manipulated into supporting the imperial interests of men like Chamberlain and Milner. With this in mind, the following section will take up the second feature of new imperialism that was identified by Marshall: increased public interest in empire.

IMPERIAL PROPAGANDA

The events of Mafeking Night that opened this unit might be seen as evidence of the popularity of imperialism. But is this the case? During the South African War the press had closely followed the progress of the British troops using special reporters on the ground. The British entered the war in October 1899 with every expectation that victory over the Boers would be quick and easy, as the Boers had no regular army and no obvious industrial base to supply their forces. The first few months of the war, however, were disastrous. One week in December was particularly bad and became known as 'Black Week'. This is how it was described by Sir Arthur Conan Doyle:

> The week which extended from December 10th to December 17th, 1899, was the blackest one known to our generation, and the most disastrous for British arms during the century. We had in the short space of seven days lost, beyond all extenuation or excuse, three separate actions. No single defeat was of vital importance in itself, but the cumulative effect occurring as they did to each of the main British forces in South Africa, was very great.
>
> (Conan Doyle, 1900, p. 83)

The Boers laid siege to three British towns: Mafeking, Kimberley and Ladysmith. Ladysmith and Kimberley were relieved by British forces in February of 1900, but Mafeking was under siege till May. The town was under the command of Colonel Baden-Powell, whose telegrams suggested that the situation in the town was fairly stable; nevertheless, the relief of Mafeking was greatly anticipated and closely watched by the newspapers in Britain. When news reached London on Friday 18 May 1900 that the siege had ended, crowds in towns and cities took to the streets to celebrate. Events were so spontaneous and popular that a new verb 'to maffick' was created and a new song 'Mother may I go and maffick, run around and hinder traffick' appeared.

Robert Baden-Powell (1857–1941) was an army officer, writer and founder of the boy-scout movement in Britain. He was born in London, one of ten children. Baden-Powell joined the British army in 1876 and spent time in India and Africa. He fought in the second Matabele War 1896–97, where he met Frederick Russell Burnham, an American who joined the army of the British South Africa Company as a scout or tracker. Burnham was one of the few to survive the Shangani Patrol in which a detachment of men led by Major Allan Wilson were cornered and killed by Ndebele fighters. He introduced Baden-Powell to skills of tracking and outdoor survival that became a key part of the scouting movement. Baden-Powell became a household name in Britain during the Boer War when, as a colonel in the British Army, he and his troops successfully held out during the siege of Mafeking in 1900. He was promoted to major-general in 1900 and charged with establishing the South African constabulary. He returned to Britain in 1902, and in 1910 he retired from the army. Baden-Powell wrote a military training manual, *Aids to Scouting*, based on his experiences in the army and it soon became a bestseller. He rewrote the book for younger readers as *Scouting for Boys* in 1908. The Scouts emerged soon after, alongside other groups such as the Boy's Brigade (formed 1883) and the Woodcraft Indians (formed 1902). The Girl Guides movement was founded in 1910 with the help of Baden-Powell's sister, Agnes Baden-Powell.

EXERCISE

Read this account of events from the *Daily Mail*, 19 May 1900. The *Daily Mail* was founded in 1896; it was sensationalist in tone and priced at half a penny so as to be affordable by the lower-middle and working classes:

> 'Mafeking is relieved!' Instantly the cry was taken up on the omibuses, and the people came clambering down in hot haste to hear the news repeated over and over again. Most of them stopped still as if it were too good to be true. Others rushed off into the byways carrying the tidings farther and farther away, all the time the streets became thicker with people cheering, shouting and singing ... Women absolutely wept for joy and men threw their arms about each other's necks – stranger's necks for the most part; but that made no difference, for Mafeking was relieved.

> (*Daily Mail*, 19 May 1900)

Now look closely at two images of Mafeking Night – Plate 21.1 in the *Visual Sources* and Figure 21.10. These images provide visual evidence of the events of Mafeking Night. How is popular jubilation at the relief of Mafeking represented in these images? What you notice about the composition of the crowd? What might you assume from the *Daily Mail* report and these images about public support for war in South Africa?

Spend about 10 minutes on this exercise.

The relief of Mafeking was celebrated with the utmost enthusiasm in Portsmouth. After "closing-time" Commercial Road was thronged with cheering crowds. By common consent the corner of Edinburgh Road was chosen as a suitable halting-place, and until long after midnight the crowd continued to exhibit the most frantic signs of joy. Men and women danced, sang, and shouted, while every man in uniform—be he sailor, soldier, marine, or stoker—was at one time or another hoisted shoulder high by his comrades and carried around amongst the shouting throng. The gallant defender of Mafeking was frequently singled out by some more than usually loud-voiced individual, and the cheers which followed the mention of the name "Baden-Powell" sent the crowd into still greater ecstasies of delight, and the cheering and "hooraying" were almost deafening. "For he's a jolly good fellow," "Rule Britannia" and "A hot time in the Transvaal to-night," were the favourite airs, but the singers were too wild with excitement to follow any one particular leader until a gang of bluejackets formed up in a ring and started the National Anthem. This supplied the climax, and for the next few minutes the din created by some three thousand throats was something terrific.

"MAFEKING DAY" IN PORTSMOUTH: COMMERCIAL ROAD AT NIGHT

Figure 21.10   Reginald Cleaver, the relief of Mafeking: celebrations in Commercial Road, Portsmouth, drawing reproduced in *The Graphic*, 26 May 1900. Photo: Mary Evans Picture Library

SPECIMEN ANSWER

Both images show the crowds to be jubilant, patriotic and spontaneous. The crowd is raucous and disorganised – there is no ordered procession or activity – but it is not threatening. In the London picture, there are characters blowing horns and whistles; in the Portsmouth picture, there appears to be singing or shouting and hats are thrown into the air. In the London image, a member of the crowd is carrying a placard with a picture of Baden-Powell, the hero of the hour. The image is also composed in a manner that suggests the crowd is 'popular'. In the Portsmouth image, there is a mixture of military personnel and male and female civilians. The crowd in the London image is composed of men, women and children from across the class spectrum. There are men and women in evening wear alongside more casually dressed men in flat caps.

The presence of such a large crowd of people suggests that the British public were interested in the war and supported the troops. The newspaper report indicates that the celebrations were spontaneous, which again implies that support was heartfelt and enthusiastic. The report and the images suggest that the news from Mafeking brought a range of people together. This is an important point. The mixture of people suggests that the British 'public' (a broad section of the nation as opposed to one or two interested parties), were genuinely interested in imperial wars.

Marshall has argued that there was nothing new about the Mafeking celebrations; similar celebrations took place on the fall of Quebec in 1759, informed by the same spirit – 'a great national deliverance after much adversity' (Marshall, 1996, pp. 52–3). Paula Krebs, however, argues that a new kind of journalism, which combined sensational reportage and popular appeal, played a key role in creating the public that celebrated on Mafeking night. Papers such as the *Daily Mail* and *The Graphic* were affordable and accessible to the lower-middle and working classes. The broad appeal of the papers brought these groups together with others to form the 'public', which was both the subject and object of its reports. As Krebs says, 'In the events of Mafeking Night we see the emergence of a British public that observers had been assuming existed all the while they were creating it' (Krebs, 1999, pp. 4–5). So how did the newspaper reports create the public response to the relief of Mafeking? Krebs argues that while historians have become adept at reading visual images of empire as a representation, rather than an accurate description, of events, all too often textual accounts are taken at face value. Instead, Krebs shows how reports combined government censorship, sensational accounts of the siege and hero worship to build up tension and emotion, which were then relieved with the relief of Mafeking. The siege was a drama played out in the pages of the press, which had successfully caught the public imagination and, for a moment, seemed to eclipse any opposition to the war.

Was there a clear attempt to persuade the public about the benefits of imperialism through propaganda?

Hobson certainly thought so. In *The Psychology of Jingoism* (1901), Hobson argued that the public were persuaded by the press, which was controlled by men closely related to those with financial interests in imperialism, that the war was being fought for the cause of civilisation against the backward Boers. The press, Hobson argued, manipulated the 'animalism' of the uneducated working classes and the naivety of the middle classes in creating a jingoistic crowd that offered unthinking and enthusiastic support for war (Krebs, 1999, p. 27). In fact, Hobson claimed, the war was motivated by financial/mining interests in South Africa who wanted to remove the Boer leaders that stood in the way of labour supply for the gold mines. The new journalism may well have attempted to whip up popular public support for the troops in the South African War, but such spontaneous public support was ephemeral. In December 1900, Emily Hobhouse went to South Africa as part of the antiwar group South African Women and Children's Distress Fund. She wrote a report about the use of concentration camps to house Boer prisoners of war that was published in June 1901. Her report and those that followed in their wake revealed that, by that end of the war, around 28,000 whites, mostly women and children, and probably around 14,000 Africans had died in camps (Krebs, 1999, p. 32). The story of the concentration camps, together with the low status of Britain's reputation abroad, caused a national scandal that seriously eroded popular support for the war. For this reason, as Marshall has conceded, the South African War was an 'imperial crisis of gigantic proportions' which exposed serious differences of opinion about the British empire (Marshall, 1996, p. 64).

this then leads to

As the example of the South African War shows, the links between imperialism, patriotism and propaganda were not straightforward. It is difficult to identify conscious and deliberate attempts by imperialists to influence public opinion. Efforts were made to teach schoolchildren of the importance of empire to the nation through their formal education and their leisure. Clubs and associations such as the Boy's Brigade (1883), the Boy Scouts (1908) and, later, the Girl Guides (1912) aimed to encourage patriotic and imperial values. The Boy Scouts movement was founded by one of the heroes of the South African War: Baden-Powell. A lot of children's literature included imperial settings and themes, but the impact of such material is difficult to assess. A small group of politicians and imperial lobbyists such as Chamberlain felt that the public must be educated into the benefits of empire to the nation. Through his speeches and writing, Chamberlain campaigned for a greater awareness of imperial values throughout Britain and the empire. On the whole, most imperial activists came from outside the ranks of government as members of societies such as the Royal Colonial Institute, which aimed to educate and inform on colonial matters. But the most pervasive forms of imperial motifs were found in popular culture: stories, adverts and music hall songs, which were diverse and difficult to associate with any one body of opinion. It is therefore difficult to know whether participation in aspects of imperial culture meant that the public actively supported new ideas about British imperialism that were promoted by men like Chamberlain.

Historians have challenged the unproblematic association between empire, the economy and politically motivated propaganda that was posited in the early twentieth century by writers such as Hobson. This recent work suggests that the relationship between popular culture and imperial policy was not at all clear. But ideas do not have to be coherent and sustained to influence the way people think about or perceive empire. The following two sections will introduce other approaches to the history of empire that use everyday sources and evidence, such as adverts, the urban landscape and museum exhibits, to see how people came to know about empire through their everyday lives.

EMPIRE, COMMERCE AND CULTURE

There are other sources that may give historians insight into the place of imperialism in popular culture. The sense that there was something new about late nineteenth-century imperialism is also informed by the saturation of British culture with imperial themes. Art, literature, music and theatre often explored imperial motifs, while exhibitions and public ceremonies demonstrated and celebrated Britain's imperial connections and created a sense that Britain was an imperial nation. In many ways this was because imperialism of the late nineteenth century corresponded with the growth of consumer culture that permeated British life more than ever before. In this section, you will consider one of the more pervasive aspects of this consumer culture, one that exploited imperial imagery extensively: the world of advertising.

EXERCISE

Find the advert for Pears' soap in the *Visual Sources*, Plate 21.6.

Until the late nineteenth century, soap tended to be manufactured locally from tallow and sold locally by weight. The industry expanded massively in the nineteenth century, leading to conglomeration; production was dominated by large businesses that advertised and branded the product to sell it nationwide. Sunlight soap, made by Lever, and Pears' soap were the market leaders. The expansion of soap production was linked to the commercial exploitation of Africa. Instead of tallow, vegetable oils were used in the new soap. Palm oil and palm kernel oil were traded from the Niger region of West Africa. British interests were negotiated by the Royal Niger Company, which obtained treaties with local rulers (Ramamurthy, 2003, p. 25).

The advert appeared in *The Graphic* on 30 July 1887. It contains an image of a group of Sudanese Muslim warriors (that the Victorians termed dervishes) looking at a rock with the words 'Pears' soap is the best' painted on them. A statement reads 'Pears' soap has been inscribed on the furthest point of British advancement' and the caption at the top reads 'The Formula of British Conquest'.

Look at the image carefully and answer the questions below.

1   Why do you think the advertisers have used this image? What is it supposed to mean?

2   How does contextual information help you to read this advert? Remind yourself of events that had taken place in Sudan around the time that this advert appeared and look again at the sentence on soap and Niger above.

Spend about 20 minutes on this exercise.

SPECIMEN ANSWER

1   On an initial view, it would seem that the image is composed to show a number of Sudanese warriors stopping in wonder and awe at a statement about Pears' soap painted on a rock. The image, taken together with the caption 'The Formula of British Conquest', suggests that trade and commerce, in this case soap manufacture, is foremost in the development of the British empire into new areas.

2   This advert appeared two years after Gordon's death at the hands of Mahdi forces. The war between the Sudanese Mahdi forces and the British in Sudan was interpreted by some as a religious war and the association between the Mahdi and slave traders was well-known. Here, the themes of religion and labour are reworked and the Sudanese warriors are seen to be worshipping British commerce. It is possible the advertisers are suggesting that commerce may be more effective than war in conquering and civilising Africa.

DISCUSSION

An initial reading of the Pears' soap advert shows the associations that were being made between soap, empire, conquest and civilisation (McClintock, 1995, p. 208). According to Ramamurthy, these associations reflect the way trade with West Africa was presented by commercial agents: 'Trade in such goods also represented the transition from slave trading to that of "legitimate commerce"' (Ramamurthy, 2003, p. 25). The kingdom of Dahomey, for instance, switched directly from slave trading with Europeans to trade in palm oil and palm kernel oil. This shift in the primary commodity of trading relations may be one of the reasons why soap advertisers exploited the theme of trade as a civilising force so extensively in the period.

Advertisements are historical documents but they do not simply reflect the ideologies of the time. The Pears' soap advertising campaign was at the forefront of a new era in advertising which used gimmicks to attract public attention to their product. Pears' was well known for manipulating images and meanings. A clearer example of this process can be seen in the 'Little black boy washes white' from the 1890s, which you can find in the *Visual Sources*, Plate 21.7. This image plays with ideas of race and progress, showing the white boy benevolently cleansing his black brother, literally helping to make him white. According to McClintock, soap advertising 'offers an allegory of imperial progress as spectacle' (McClintock, 1995, 214). By this she means that advertising plays with ideas of imperial progress to draw attention to the product.

John MacKenzie has noted:

> It is perhaps difficult for us, jaded by the printed word and the omnipresent electronic media, to comprehend fully the impact of these materials. There seems to have been a craving for visual representations of the world, of events, and of the great and the famous, which a large number of agencies and commercial companies sought to satisfy in the period from the 1870s to the First World War. New advertising techniques were central to this activity, and companies creating and supplying the new tastes were concerned to

sell not just their own product, but the worked system which produced it.

(Quoted in Ramamurthy, 2003, p. 2; see also Hobsbawn, 1997, p. 65)

Were these adverts selling imperialism as well as soap?

Empire was a popular theme with advertisers and publishers because it was familiar to audiences. As you saw earlier in the unit, the public would be reading about imperial adventures in newspapers and books. John Springhall had argued that the 'little wars' of empire that took place in almost every year of Queen Victoria's reign after 1870 provided ample material for stories of adventure in exotic landscapes with generals in imperial armies made into popular heroes (Springhall, 1986, p. 49). In the late nineteenth century, illustrated newspapers like *The Graphic* and the *Illustrated London News* sent artists and reporters to the front line. Their pictures and reports provided first-hand accounts of imperial adventure to their readers. According to Hobson, such reports were central to imperialism's hold on the public imagination: 'hero-worship and sensational glory, adventure and the sporting spirit: current history falsified in coarse flaring colours, for the direct stimulation of the combative instincts' (Springhall, 1986, p. 49). The Sudanese campaign referred to in the Pears' advert would be familiar to the public. The vicious nature of the fighting in Sudan was retold by reporters such as Winston Churchill with salacious detail. As Rudyard Kipling wryly stated:

> The Sudan campaign was a picturesque one, and lent itself to vivid word painting. Now and again a 'special' managed to get slain – which was not altogether a disadvantage to the paper that employed him – and more often the hand-to-hand nature of the fighting allowed of miraculous escapes which were worth telegraphing home at eighteen pence the word.
>
> (Quoted in Springhall, 1986, p. 57)

Only the *Daily Mail's* correspondent George Steevens had reported the extent of the ruthless slaughter of the Mahdi's men by British artillery (Springhall, 1986, p. 59).

It is difficult for the historian to know how the public interpreted these images but we can assume that they were familiar to many people. The repetition of these imperial themes in adverts to sell products may even suggest that audiences felt positive about empire. According to Marshall, 'Expectations that the public would buy articles to which imperial connotations had been attached is, however, important evidence that the British people in general were presumed to be well disposed to empire and likely to respond enthusiastically to allusions to it'(Marshall, 1996, p. 62). The use of imperial images in adverts also demonstrates the interconnections between the economy and empire: the British public encountered empire through everyday products such as tea, soap and sugar, and advertisers were keen to exploit this. Is it the case that advertisers were motivated to garner public support for the empire in the interests of trade? Again, Marshall has an opinion on this, 'Writers and

[handwritten marginal note:] Don't forget the Crimea before that!

publishers presumably took their own commercial decisions when they gave their popular songs or children's stories an imperial setting. Advertisers were concerned with selling their goods, not with propagating imperialist ideology' (Marshall, 1996, p. 62). However, as these imperial adverts demonstrate, the empire was big business and ideas about empire are very difficult to separate from economics of empire.

EMPIRE AND THE PRODUCTION OF KNOWLEDGE

The late nineteenth century was, more than any other period, associated with the production of spectacles of empire designed for the education and entertainment of the 'masses'. Museum displays and imperial exhibitions became increasingly popular formats in which knowledge about empire and nation was displayed, and imperial trade was promoted. They were sites in which the economics of empire and ideas about empire came together. According to Hoffenberg, 'exhibition ceremonies complemented other English and colonial rituals; they created and reflected the idea, images, and fantasies necessary for nationalism and imperialism' (Hoffenberg, 2001, p. 243).

After the success of the Great Exhibition of 1851, various events were held in European cities to display national wealth, to promote trade and to educate the masses in the benefits of empire. Offering a combination of displays of products, pageants and human showcases, the exhibitions were designed to show the whole gamut of life in other places. They were often funded and promoted by a broad section of middle-class society. According to Coombes 'The mainstay of both museum ethnography and of exhibitions in Britain were industrial capitalists, entrepreneurs and civil servants in the colonial service, together with the semi-professionals of learned societies like the national and regional geographical societies and the Anthropological Institute' (Coombes, 1994, p. 214). As such, these events tended to represent a number of perspectives on empire from pseudo-scientific ideas of race to stalls that displayed some of the produce of empire. Particularly important elements of these exhibitions were the human showcases in which people from the empire were displayed to crowds of visitors. The displaying of mock up 'native villages' complete with natives became popular after they were successfully used to attract the crowds at the 1889 Paris Exposition. What is so interesting about these exhibitions is the way they brought together imperial economic interests and ideas about race and nation.

In 1899, the Empress Theatre in Earl's Court hosted one such exhibition 'Savage South Africa, a vivid realistic and picturesque representation of life in the wilds of Africa'. The spectacle was organised by Imre Kiralfy, a Hungarian entrepreneur who was the key figure behind a large number of similar exhibitions in the 1890s and early 1900s, as part of the Greater Britain Exhibition, intended to promote trade by displaying colonial goods.

'Savage South Africa' was presented to the public as a 'sight never previously presented in Europe, a horde of savages direct from their kraals [village enclosures], who reenacted scenes from African life involving "savage" attacks on white settlements' (see Figure 21.11). In effect, the troop re-enacted some of the skirmishes between 'British, Boer and Black'. Of particular interest were enactments of the confrontations that occurred as Cecil Rhodes pursued his 'right' to territory taken from Lobengula, the Ndebele king – an area rich in resources. The British South Africa Company took the Ndebele heartlands in 1893. They looted cattle and land, and imposed taxes through a new and very unpopular police force. A re-enactment was given of the 1896 uprising in Ndebele against BSAC company rule in which Ndebele warriors attacked a white settler homestead, killing 145 whites (Marks, 1997, p. 446). A particularly popular re-enactment was of the so-called Shangani Patrol, in which a volunteer Rhodesian force led by Major Forbes went out to capture Lobengula in 1893. Twelve men, including Forbes's subordinate Major Allan Wilson, were separated from the main group and defeated. The incident became a part of Rhodesian mythology, the twelve troops depicted in stories as singing 'God Save the Queen' as they were cut down by Ndebele warriors (Greenhalgh, 1988, p. 97; see also Shephard, 1986, p. 98).

EXERCISE

Read the press report of the Savage South Africa Exhibition in the article entitled 'The Greater Britain Exhibition', which appeared in *The Times* on 9 May 1899 and is reproduced in the secondary sources on the course website. What do you notice about the way South Africans and British are represented?

Spend about 20 minutes on this exercise.

SPECIMEN ANSWER

The reporter views the Africans with curiosity, as though they are a spectacle presented for amusement, which is, of course, the very way they are presented to the audience. The movements and appearance of the Africans are commented on in much the same way as those of the elephants, horses and monkeys. For example, 'the blacks squat about, crawl in and out of the narrow hut-doors, and appear to be getting accustomed to the unfamiliar surroundings.' There is some discussion of the 'native' African warriors as primitive but brave, whose skills were no match for the discipline and technological sophistication of the British. For example, the reference to the Maxim gun notes that 'Those who have never before seen one of these deadly arms of precision in use will have no difficulty in understanding how effective such a weapon is against hordes of undisciplined men, however brave they may be.' According to the reporter the British sense of fairness is also shown in the audience's ability to recognise bravery in the African soldier.

DISCUSSION

To some extent these representations drew on ideas of race that were already in circulation in the nineteenth century. Greenhalgh has shown how existing ideas about race were taken up and applied in exhibitions to construct theories of racial hierarchies (Greenhalgh, 1998, p. 96). The exhibitions became theatres in which racial differences were constructed and confirmed with the new sciences of anthropology and ethnography, which gave authority and respectability to racist ideas. But, as you saw with the report on 'Savage South Africa', these spectacles showed that ideas of Britishness and Africaness were often intertwined. British superiority was defined in opposition to Africans. Similar ideas can be seen in the speeches and writings of imperialists.

Figure 21.11   William T. Maud, 'A Peek at the Natives', Savage South Africa at Earl's Court, 1899, pen and washes on paper, 35 x 26.7 cm. Photo: © Private Collection / © Michael Graham-Stewart / The Bridgeman Art Library

EXERCISE

Look at Anthology Document 6.4, 'Britain's acquisition of Egypt in 1882', which is a speech made by Earl Cromer. Can you identify the ways that Cromer has employed notions of race in producing ideas about British imperial destiny? Look also at Anthology Document 6.3, 'Joseph Chamberlain, speech on "The true conception of empire", 1897'. How does Chamberlain employ ideas of race to justify British imperialism?

Spend about 10 minutes on this exercise.

SPECIMEN ANSWER

Cromer argues that the British had to occupy Egypt because the Egyptians were incapable of running the country themselves. He claims that only the British had the sophistication to govern such a strategically important country. Chamberlain also argues that British superiority compels Britain to spread the benefits of civilisation to other countries.

DISCUSSION

It is difficult to measure the influence of ideas of race on the process of imperial expansion. Christine Bolt has argued that ideas of race provided 'a perfect rationale for imperialist ventures once undertaken, and fashioned a "colonial mentality" to which the establishments of colonial government merely put the final seal' (Bolt, 1971, p. 218). Attitudes to race were certainly diverse, but they appear to be hardening in the late nineteenth century in response to imperial conflict and in line with theories of human progress such as social Darwinism. Perhaps ideas of race and nation were not enough in themselves to motivate imperialism, but they certainly fuelled further interest in theories of race and national identity, and, as some of Chamberlain's speeches demonstrate, ideas of evolutionary destiny provided justification for imperial ventures.

EMPIRE AND BRITISHNESS

As the debate on imperialism and propaganda shows, imperialism is a process of extension and expansion overseas but it also had an impact at home. In the late nineteenth century, empire was a key theme in British culture: empire was a feature of art and literature, ceremonies and spectacles. As such, this imperial culture reflected and constructed what many people in Britain thought about themselves and those that were colonised. This section will ask you to think about the significance of these ideas of imperialism: In what ways did ideas about the British nation and the colony shape imperialism in the late nineteenth century and in what ways did imperialism shape ideas of Britishness?

More recent studies of imperialism have been powerfully influenced by the work of Edward Said. His book *Orientalism* argued that ideas of empire did more than simply produce a justifying ideology for imperialism. Said used the term 'orientalism' to describe the 'modern political-intellectual culture' that constructed ideas about the west in relation to the non-west and made empire possible (Said, 1978, p. 12). Said studied the range of opinions and descriptions of empire to see how a discourse about empire shaped the nexus of knowledge and power central to empire: put simply, in producing ideas about other people in far-flung places, the British ('us') produced the ability to dominate 'them' (Said, 1978, p. 32). In a subsequent work, *Culture and Imperialism*, Said noted the vast range of people, in both the empire and the metropolis, who contributed to this imperial discourse: 'scholars, administrators, travelers, traders, parliamentarians, merchants, novelists, theorists, speculators, adventurers, visionaries, poets, and every variety of outcast and misfit in the outlying possessions of these two imperial powers, each of who contributed to the formation of a colonial actuality existing at the heart of metropolitan life' (Said, 1993, p. 8).

EXERCISE

Read this extract from Said,

> Neither imperialism nor colonialism is a simple act of accumulation and acquisition. Both are supported and perhaps even impelled by impressive ideological formations that include notions that certain territories and people require and beseech domination, as well as forms of knowledge affiliated with domination: the vocabulary of classic nineteenth century imperial culture is plentiful with words and concepts as 'inferior' or 'subject races', 'subordinate peoples', 'dependency', 'expansion', and 'authority.
>
> (Said, 1993, p. 8)

What does Said mean?

Spend about 5 minutes on this exercise.

SPECIMEN ANSWER

Said is arguing here that the knowledge about empire was not benign. In effect, nineteenth-century ideas of other people in empire, such as the African or the Indian, actively produced differences and power. The key to Said's argument is that knowledge about peoples overseas is not innocent but connected to the process of holding power over them.

DISCUSSION

According to Said, the construction of knowledge about peoples and places in ideas of empire is not necessarily undertaken in full consciousness – however, the knowledge of other people produced in imperial culture is not innocent or objective because it is produced by human beings who were embedded in colonial history and relationships. Said and other post-colonial thinkers argue that a careful analysis of language and images makes it possible for the historian to see connections between the ideas and institutions through structures of thinking. In this way, we can see imperialists such as Chamberlain and Cromer as part of a broader imperial culture that saw distinctions between races and the imperial motivation as acceptable and normal – as much a part of British identity as a way of identifying others.

knew + exploited those differences

In his influential book *Orientalism*, Said argued that oppositions are established in ideas about empire that come to define the colonised and the colonisers: 'if colonized people are irrational, Europeans are rational; if the former are barbaric, sensual, and lazy, Europe is civilization itself, with its sexual appetites under control and its dominant ethic that of hard work' (Loomba, 1998, p. 47). There are, as always, criticisms of Said's approach. Some historians have argued that he does not give enough attention to resistance to these ideas, both at home and in the colonies. It is unlikely that the colonised or the colonisers uncritically accepted ideas about race and nation. Another very important criticism of Said's work is the way that it simplifies the many and various attitudes to race evident in the late nineteenth century. Cannadine has argued that rather than ideas of us and them, the British empire involved 'the replication of sameness and similarities originating from home' as much as 'the insistence on difference and dissimilarities originating from overseas'(Cannadine, 2001, p. xix). For Cannadine, social hierarchies cut right through ideas of race and nation in the British empire.

Nevertheless, Said's work has opened up awareness among historians that ideas and expressions of the British nation are profoundly influenced by empire and that a full understanding of imperial history needs to consider the interconnections between the history of the metropole and the periphery, and between popular ideas and imperial policy. Said has made this point in relation to British and French imperialism:

> Who in India or Algeria today can confidently separate out the British or French component of the past from present actualities; and who in Britain or France can draw a clear circle around British London or French Paris that would exclude the impact of India and Algeria upon these two imperial cities?
>
> (Said, 1993, p. 15)

What does Said mean by this? And why does he feel it is important to say it? Your work on the DVD will help you to consider this question.

DVD exercise

Now turn to the DVD 3 Section 1 and do the exercises on imperial London.

The DVD exercises demonstrate that ideas about empire impacted on the urban landscape, particularly in the design and layout of the capital city. Reflecting Said's argument, the design and layout of central London can be seen to be self-consciously conceived to reflect imperial greatness. But, as work by Felix Driver and David Gilbert has pointed out, the landscape of 'imperial London' was as much concerned with defining Britishness in relation to other European countries as it was with reflecting British civility, commerce and ceremony in relation to colonised nations (Driver and Gilbert, 1998, p. 13). For example, after its Industrial Exhibition of 1896, Berlin termed itself a 'world city' or *Weltstadt*, and, like London, its architecture was self-consciously designed to reflect imperial themes. You will find further information about the DVD in the *Media Guide*.

Spend about 2 hours on these exercises.

EXERCISE

As your work on this unit and DVD 3 has shown, imperial culture was diverse. How, then, did it inform imperialism and nationalism in the late nineteenth century? This final exercise will help you to bring all the ideas we have discussed together by reading an article by P. J. Marshall written in 1995. In it, Marshall considers the state of the study of imperial Britain as it was then. In so doing, he provides a useful overview of some of the scholarship on British imperialism.

Read the article 'Imperial Britain' by P. J. Marshall, which you can find in the secondary sources on the course website. Use the questions below to help you pull out the salient points of the four main parts of the article. Do not worry about detail; just note one or two general points in answer to the questions.

1   Look at section I of the article. According to Marshall, did imperialism transform Britain's institutions?

2   Turn to section II. How, according to Marshall, did imperialism help to define Britishness?

3   Now consider section III. How was this sense of Britishness defined by imperialism?

4   In section IV, how does Marshall see the traditions of imperialism being reflected in ideas about the British empire?

Spend about 2 hours on this exercise.

SPECIMEN ANSWER

1   Not really. Empire was prominent in political debate from 1880 to 1906, otherwise it was not so. This limited debate might indicate that a commitment to empire was an 'underlying priority'. Imperialism had some impact on the ~~the~~ ~~the~~ monarchy, churches and the army, all of which took on an international role. On the other hand, Marshall notes an extraordinary resistance of the political institutions of Britain to adapt to reflect an imperial role.

2   Marshall argues that imperialism has been a considerable part of the cultural life of Britain from at least the eighteenth century. Art and literature, popular entertainment and education actively engaged with imperial themes and not simply in the production of propaganda. This culture included Scottish, Irish and English people and, in the production of a sense of 'Britishness' in opposition to other European people and the colonised, this culture helped to integrate the United Kingdom.

3   Marshall argues against the idea that there was one hegemonic idea of Britishness that was, in effect, metropolitan Englishness writ large. Instead, he argues that the diversity of imperialism enabled it to accommodate a vast range of British people.

4   Marshall notes that there are two general imperial traditions: authoritarian and libertarian. While the former has been more closely identified with the late nineteenth century, the latter was more typical of attitudes to imperialism, in part because libertarian attitudes to imperialism gave it moral sanction. As Marshall says, this tradition may be self-deluding but it nevertheless reflects what many people perceived the British empire to be.

DISCUSSION

How does Marshall's approach help us to understand the relationship between imperialism and the formation of a national British identity? On the one hand, as Marshall notes, despite the central importance of imperialism to Britain's industrial and political history in the nineteenth century, its institutions remained largely inward looking. Many still study British industrial, urban and political history without making any reference to empire. On the other hand, an idea of empire was central to definitions of Britishness in the nineteenth century. So, while the experience of empire did not transform Britain it did transform ideas of Britishness.

In turn, as the work in this unit has shown, ideas of Britishness and what the British nation should be like did influence and inform the imperial designs of individuals such as Chamberlain and Milner, men who were very much associated with the drive for imperial unity. Such campaigns were promoted by organisations such as the Imperial Federation League that included academics, politicians, colonial administrators and businessmen, and which produced arguments in support of imperial unity that combined ideas of racial superiority, nationalism, practical politics and economics to justify their campaigns. But, in practice, their campaigns came to nothing: there was little agreement on the nature of such an imperial union, what its authority would be and how it would be funded.

CONCLUSION

We began this unit by questioning whether or not 'new imperialism' was a useful tool for understanding the more aggressive kind of colonisation that took place in the late nineteenth century, particularly in Africa. The usefulness of the term depends on the extent to which studies focus on common themes in the expansion of the period, such as the role of finance capital and the way events resulted in British government intervention. Other approaches, such as the one favoured by Andrew Porter, prefer to emphasise the particularity of each case of imperial intervention to argue that no common causes or motives can be identified. There is nevertheless still the need to explain why the imperialism of the period was felt to be new and different, and how imperialists such as Seeley, Cromer and Chamberlain were able, for a time, to gain an audience for their view. Debates about the British empire were diverse and wide-ranging in the late nineteenth century, as is evidenced in the saturation of British culture with imperial themes. But, although this culture may not necessarily have transformed the institutions of government, it did inform ideas about Britishness in opposition to other European nations and colonised peoples. In turn, as the writing of men such as Chamberlain and Cromer demonstrated, ideas of Britishness informed attitudes to empire. In this way, the unit demonstrates how the course themes of state formation, and beliefs and ideologies are closely related in the study of nations and imperialism. As the example of the South African War shows, the theme of producers and consumers is closely intertwined with the other themes. The following unit will explore in greater detail the complex relations that linked economic and imperial expansion.

REFERENCES

Bolt, C. (1971) *Victorian Attitudes to Race*, London, Routledge and Kegan Paul.

Cain, P.J. (2002) *Hobson and Imperialism: New Liberalism, and Finance 1887–1938*, New York, Oxford University Press.

Cannadine, D. (2001) *Ornamentalism*, London, Penguin.

Conan Doyle, A. (1902) *The Great Boer War*, London, Smith, Elder and Co.

Coombes, A. (1994) *Reinventing Africa. Museums, Material Culture and Popular Imagination in Late Victorian and Edwardian England*, New Haven, Yale University Press.

Driver, F. and Gilbert, D. (1998)'Heart of empire? Landscape, space and performance in imperial London' *Environment and Planning D: Society and Space*, vol. 16, no.1, pp. 11–28.

Gallagher, J. and Robinson, R. (1953) 'The imperialism of free trade' in *Economic History Review*, vol. 6, no.1, pp. 1–15.

Greenhalgh, P. (1988) *Ephemeral Vistas: The Expositions Universelles, Great Exhibitions and World's Fairs, 1851–1939*, Manchester, Manchester University Press.

Hall, C. (1992) *White, Male and Middle-Class. Explorations in Feminism and History*, Cambridge, Polity Press.

Hobsbawn, E. (1997) *Age of Empire, 1875–1914*, 4th edn, London, Weidenfeld & Nicolson.

Hobson, J.A. (1901) *The Psychology of Jingoism*, London, Grant Richards.

Hobson, J.A. (1988 [1902]) *Imperialism: A Study*, 3rd edn, London, Unwin Hyman.

Hoffenberg, P. (2001) *An Empire on Display: English, Indian, and Australian Exhibitions from the Crystal Palace to the Great War*, Berkeley, University of California Press.

Krebs, P. (1999) *Gender, Race and the Writing of Empire. Public Discourse and the Boer War*, Cambridge, Cambridge University Press.

Loomba, A. (1998) *Colonialism/Postcolonialism*, London, Routledge.

McClintock, A. (1995) *Imperial Leather: Race, Gender and Sexuality in the Colonial Conquest*, London, Routledge.

MacKenzie, J. (1984) *Propaganda and Empire. The Manipulation of British Public Opinion, 1880–1960*, Manchester, Manchester University Press.

MacKenzie, J. (ed) (1986) *Imperialism and Popular Culture*, Manchester, Manchester University Press.

Marks, S. (1997) 'Southern and central Africa, 1886–1910' in Oliver and Sanderson (1997).

Marshall, P.J. (ed.) (1996) *Cambridge Illustrated History of the British Empire*, Cambridge, Cambridge University Press.

Mitchell, T. (1988) *Colonising Egypt,* Berkeley, University of California Press.

Oliver, R. and Sanderson, G.N. (eds) (1997) *The Cambridge History of Africa*, vol. 6, Cambridge, Cambridge University Press.

Porter, B. (1996) *The Lion's Share: A Short History of British Imperialism, 1850–1995*, 3rd edn, London, Longman.

Ramamurthy, A. (2003) *Imperial Persuaders. Images of Africa and Asia in British Advertising*, Manchester University Press, Manchester.

Robinson, R. and Gallagher, J. (1981) *Africa and the Victorians: The Official Mind of Imperialism*, 2nd edn, Basingstoke, Macmillan.

Said, E. (1978) *Orientalism*, London, Penguin.

Said, E. (1994) *Culture and Imperialism*, London, Vintage.

Sanderson, G.N. (1997a) 'The European partition of Africa: origins and dynamics' in Oliver and Sanderson (1997).

Sanderson, G.N. (1997b) 'The Nile basin and the eastern Horn, 1870–1908' in Oliver and Sanderson (1997).

Seeley, J.R., (1883) *The Expansion of England*, London, Macmillan.

Shephard, B. (1986) 'Showbiz imperialism: the case of Peter Lobengula' in MacKenzie (1986), pp. 94–112.

Springhall, J.O. (1986) '"Up guards and at them!": British imperialism and popular art, 1880–1914' in MacKenzie (1986), pp.49–72.

Waites, B. (1999) *Europe and the Third World: From Colonization to Decolonization*, Basingstoke, Macmillan.

Robin Mackie

INTRODUCTION

This unit will focus on the economics of empire, and, in particular, of the British empire in the second half of the nineteenth century. As such, the course theme of producers and consumers is central. Of the other two themes, beliefs and ideologies will only figure briefly when we consider how contemporaries thought about the economy. The unit will start by introducing some of the debates surrounding the economics of British imperialism. It will then go on to explore how empire and imperial trade shaped economic structures and urban society in late nineteenth-century Britain. For this, it will use a case study of one town: the city of Dundee in eastern Scotland, and its close connection with jute, a fibre grown in Bengal that was widely used for packaging in the nineteenth century. Exploring such a huge subject as empire through an apparently rather narrow study may seem unusual, but this approach is one historians often use to examine broad issues in greater detail. The case study also makes it possible to look at a range of sources used by economic and social historians.

The unit is divided into four sections. The first explores how historians have written about the relationship between Britain's economic and imperial expansion, and discusses a very influential work on the subject – P. J. Cain and A. G. Hopkins's *British Imperialism*. The second section introduces Dundee and explains the rise of the jute industry and its later difficulties. Next, the unit explores how the industry was organised and, by looking at the example of one firm, how firms survived in highly competitive and volatile trading conditions. The fourth section considers the impact of jute on Dundee, focusing on how it was perceived by contemporaries. Finally, the conclusion will attempt to link the particular back to the general, by tying the Dundee case study to the main issues raised by Cain and Hopkins.

INTRODUCING THE HISTORICAL DEBATE: INDUSTRY, EMPIRE AND GENTLEMEN CAPITALISTS

Industry and empire

That there should be a link between Britain's early industrialisation and the British empire is something that we take for granted, unexamined. In the late eighteenth and early nineteenth centuries, Britain was the first country to industrialise, giving it a dominant position in the world economy that was to last for more than a century. During the same period, it acquired the largest empire ever. Surely there must be some relationship between these two developments?

In a textbook entitled *Industry and Empire,* first published in 1968, Eric Hobsbawm, discussed this relationship (there is an extract from his book in the secondary sources on the course website). He starts by highlighting the importance of the Industrial Revolution and the power it briefly gave Britain:

> There was a moment in the world's history when Britain can be described, if we are not too pedantic, as its only workshop, its only massive importer and exporter, its only carrier, its only imperialist, almost its only foreign investor ... Much of this monopoly was simply due to the loneliness of the pioneer ... When other countries industrialized, it ended automatically.
>
> (Hobsbawm, 1968, pp. 13–14)

He then considers the unique role in the world economy that this situation created. Britain became

> the agency of economic interchange between the advanced and the backward, the industrial and the primary-producing, the metropolitan and the colonial or quasi-colonial regions of the world ... [T]he world economy of nineteenth-century capitalism developed as a single system of free flows, in which the international transfers of capital or commodities passed largely through British hands and institutions, in British ships between the continents, and were calculated in terms of the pound sterling.
>
> (Hobsbawm, 1968, pp. 13–14)

Hobsbawm goes on to point out that Britain was quite prepared to force poorer regions of the world to participate in this economic system. Yet his emphasis in this passage is not on coercion, but on Britain's central role in the world trading system: it is this role, rather than Britain's overseas dominions, that is presented as central to empire. In Block 4 you learnt about the importance of international trade to Britain. Britain long remained the world's most important international trader, exchanging, broadly speaking, manufactured goods for raw materials and foodstuffs. Yet, throughout the nineteenth century, most British exports did not go to the empire and most British imports did not come from it. For some foreign countries – Argentina is an oft-cited example – trade with Britain and, later, investment by Britain dominated the economy. As a result, such countries were very sensitive to British wishes and historians have used the term 'informal empire' to describe this British sphere of influence beyond the boundaries of the formal empire. Yet, on the whole, Britain did not use this influence to enforce exclusive trading agreements. From the 1820s on, British policy at home was to lower tariffs, and abroad too it encouraged free trade. Britain's early industrialisation gave it such an advantage that free trade made British goods competitive in most markets.

This way of looking at empire therefore captures an important dimension of Britain's imperial history. Where it is less helpful is in explaining territorial expansion. As you know from Unit 21, the last decades of the nineteenth century saw Britain acquire many new colonies, but it is quite difficult to show, even in the case of so valuable a colony as South Africa, that this had economic causes. Many of the new colonies were of very limited economic value. Moreover, the late nineteenth century was precisely the period when Britain's industrial leadership was coming under challenge. Was territorial expansion perhaps defensive, because informal empire was no longer enough? Did Britain acquire colonies precisely because its manufacturers were no longer so dominant?

The Cain and Hopkins thesis

In the early 1990s, the debates about the economic dimension to British imperialism were transformed by the work of two economic historians, P. J. Cain and A. G. Hopkins. In two massive volumes (*British Imperialism. Innovation and Expansion, 1688–1914* and *British Imperialism. Crisis and Deconstruction, 1914–1990*) they reviewed the entire history of the British empire from the Glorious Revolution to the fall of Mrs Thatcher (Cain and Hopkins, 1993a,b).

I would like you to read two reviews of their books: one by Martin Lynn, which appeared in the *English Historical Review* and one by David Cannadine, in *Past & Present*. Book reviews are an important part of academic journals and indeed of intellectual debate. At one level, they function as an information service: academics turn to reviews to find out about new books. It is therefore important that they include a fair summary of the contents. But a good review should do more than describe: it should also set the book in context (how does it fit with what has previously been written?) and evaluate it (how well does it achieve its aims and the needs of the field?). A 'review article', such as that by Cannadine, may be an extended essay that engages with the book's central arguments. Book reviews can therefore be an effective way to obtain an overview of the main arguments of a book and the questions it raises.

In the following section, I would like you to read and analyse the reviews by Martin Lynn and David Cannadine, which you will find in the secondary sources on the course website. Reading the articles and working on the two exercises is likely to take you about 2 hours. You will return to the points given in the specimen answers in a later exercise.

EXERCISE

Read the review by Martin Lynn, 'Review of British imperialism', and sections I and II of that by David Cannadine, 'The empire strikes back', and consider the question: what do they see as the key points in Cain and Hopkins's argument? Try to pick out a few key issues and build your answer around them.

Spend about 75 minutes on this exercise.

SPECIMEN ANSWER

1   *Empire is central to British history.* Lynn and Cannadine emphasise that Cain and Hopkins are writing about both British and imperial history. Each starts by placing *British Imperialism* in the context of debates about empire. In describing these debates, explicit links are made between theories about empire and what was happening to the empire at the time. Lynn starts with the decline of the old-

style imperial history during the 1950s (the period of decolonisation), and refers to the 'Area Studies' movement of the 1960s and 1970s, which shifted the focus away from Europe to the regions colonised. Cannadine provides rather more detail on the various theories of imperialism, but also notes that the subject went out of fashion in the 1970s. Both reviews place Cain and Hopkins's work in the context of a renewed interest in the history of empire, an interest in 'the reintegrating of the metropole into the history of Empire' (Lynn).

2   *The British empire was more than a territorial empire, it was a global economic system centred on and dominated by Britain.* Lynn and Cannadine both highlight that, in discussing empire, Cain and Hopkins are not only talking about the territories that Britain ruled, but also areas of influence, such as Latin America, China and the Ottoman empire. As Lynn puts it '[Cain and Hopkins] stress the need ... to examine the totality of British influence, formal and informal, around the globe'. In this, therefore, they follow Hobsbawm.

3   *British policy was shaped not by industry, but by 'gentlemanly capitalism'.* Both reviews emphasise the importance Cain and Hopkins attach to the financial sector. During the eighteenth century, 'a new class of merchants, financiers and businessmen, ... established themselves as junior partners to the ruling aristocracy' (Cannadine). Over time, these mercantile and aristocratic elites became increasingly integrated. The term 'gentlemanly capitalism' is used by Cain and Hopkins to denote the alliance between landed interests and the City of London. 'Gentlemanly capitalists' shared values and attitudes, and moved in the same social circles. With direct access to Britain's governing elite, it is their influence that explains the chronology and direction of Britain's imperial expansion. By contrast, industrialists remained provincial, socially inferior, and politically ineffective. As a result, promoting and safeguarding investments overseas was more important to the government than acquiring raw materials or markets.

4   *We need to rethink the conventional chronology of British empire.* Whereas historians used to contrast developments in the eighteenth and nineteenth centuries, Cain and Hopkins stress continuity. More surprisingly, they do not see decline setting in from the 1870s on. Instead, British expansion after 1850 was that of a 'dynamic and ambitious power' (quoted by Lynn). Far from being defensive, British expansion at the turn of the century was a sign of strength. Nor did 1914 mark a turning point; Cannadine notes that in the interwar years, and even after 1945, Britain's 'gentlemanly capitalists' were still seeking to use the empire to their advantage.

DISCUSSION

I have asked you to identify a few points from what are already very condensed summaries. Inevitably, we will have formulated points differently, but I hope you identified some of the same issues. Both Lynn and Cannadine emphasise the important contribution that Cain and Hopkins have made to debates about empire (some of this debate will be familiar to you from Unit 21). At the same time, there have also been criticisms of their arguments. In the second half of his article, Cannadine discusses some of the most persistent concerns: let us look at these now.

EXERCISE

Please turn now to sections III and IV of Cannadine's article and identify his major criticisms.

Spend about 45 minutes on this exercise.

SPECIMEN ANSWER

In section III, Cannadine raises three concerns about their arguments:

A   *How useful is the concept of 'gentlemanly capitalism'?* Cannadine questions the sharp distinction Cain and Hopkins draw between manufacturing and finance. Can one really talk of an 'industrial sector' and a 'financial service sector' as coherent and distinct groups? Did industry speak with one voice? Is it really possible to categorise businessmen as either 'industry' or 'finance'? Cannadine asks the same question as Porter (see Unit 21, p. 28): were there really 'close and constant connections' between finance and government which explain imperial policy?

B   *How well does the theory fit the non-English nations in the United Kingdom?* Cannadine notes that Cain and Hopkins do not really discuss whether Scotland, Wales or Ireland, or, indeed, the English provinces, fit into this thesis. For, he argues, the empire provided many opportunities for individuals from outside the charmed circle of the 'gentlemanly capitalists'. Why do we talk of *English* gentlemen and a *British* empire, he asks?

C   *Does the theory fit certain periods better than others?* Despite the titles of the books, Cannadine feels that the coverage of the eighteenth century is inadequate and is not convinced that their thesis really explains the end of empire. Indeed, he argues that the thesis is too focused on the last quarter of the nineteenth century.

He raises a further point in section IV:

D   *Is the whole theory simply too mono-causal and, perhaps, rather dated?* In section IV, Cannadine raises his most sweeping criticism. Historians must simplify to understand, but have Cain and Hopkins been too brutal in forcing so complex a phenomenon as the rise and fall of the British empire into one explanation? Cannadine finishes by suggesting that 'the Empire was always an imaginative construct, existing as much (or more) in the minds of men and women as it existed on the ground or on the map.' Are the questions that Cain and Hopkins are asking simply old-fashioned?

DISCUSSION

Many of the points made by Cannadine are ones raised by other reviewers (you may, for instance, have noticed that Lynn also notes that the significance of 'gentlemanly capitalists' has been questioned, and this indeed is one part of the thesis that has been hotly contested). Cannadine's comments in section IV also link to debates you encountered in Unit 21, including Porter's article challenging explanations for the Boer War that rely on economic causes (such as Hobson's), or the focus on the culture of empire by some historians (such as John Mackenzie). Cannadine's concerns about chronology are also significant. In particular, historians now attach a great deal of importance to the expansion of the British Empire, particularly in India, in the period of the Napoleonic Wars. This, however, was not the imperialism of free trade, but was driven by military power, the desire to increase tax revenues, and mercantilist economic ideas (Bayly, 1989).

Nevertheless, even if many historians have not agreed with all or part of Cain and Hopkins's theory, few would deny that it has provided an enormous stimulus to debate. Our understanding of broad historical processes is enhanced by such bold theories. At the same time, history is also about the particular. How well do broad theories explain individual cases? Do more in-depth studies confirm, develop or even challenge them?

In the rest of this unit, the focus will be on one town, Dundee, and the role played by empire in its economic and social development. Cain and Hopkins argue that empire was about the metropolis as well as the colonies: how well does their theory help us understand Dundee? In working your way through the unit, therefore, I would like you to keep in mind what you have read about the Cain and Hopkins thesis and jot down any points that strike you. Does their work provide insights? Are there points that do not fit? At the end of the unit, we will consider how this debate has added to our understanding of Dundee and empire.

DUNDEE AND THE JUTE INDUSTRY

Why jute? Why Dundee?

To British people in 1900 – and for long afterwards – Dundee was associated with one product: jute. Dundee was 'Juteopolis' – synonymous with its main industry. This association of place and product was not unusual. We still link Clydebank with ships, Sheffield with steel, Stoke-on-Trent with pottery, even if such industries have now dwindled to a fraction of their former size or disappeared completely. Such associations reflect the extent of regional specialisation in Britain in the industrial era. But Dundee's association with jute was an unusually close one. Throughout the late nineteenth century, over half of Dundee's workforce worked in the textile sector, which, from the 1860s on, was dominated by jute (Rodger, 1985, p. 37). The industry was also extremely concentrated. Raw jute was produced in significant quantities in only one region of the world: the deltas of the Ganges and Brahmaputra rivers in Bengal in India (see Figures 22.1 and 22.2). And for a short period – long finished by 1900 – Dundee and the surrounding district had a near monopoly on its manufacture. As a local merchant put it 'Dundee supplied the whole world'.

This achievement was all the more astonishing considering the distances involved. Even after the completion of the Suez Canal in 1869, Calcutta (Kolkata), the main city and port of Bengal, was over 9000 miles from Dundee. Nor was the jute industry unimportant: as world trade grew in the nineteenth century it became an essential commodity. Jute was the cheapest of fibres, but it was tough. As such it was the ideal packing material. Jute bagging and jute sacks were used to carry cotton from the American South, grain from the Great Plains and Argentina, coffee from the East Indies and Brazil, wool from Australia, sugar from the Caribbean and nitrates from Chile. How did Dundee come to play such an important role?

Cutting jute (standing)

Figure 22.1 Photographer unknown, Cutting jute, West Bengal, *c.*1900, photograph, 19.4 x 13.4 cm. Photo: Courtesy of University of Dundee Archive Services.

Loading Jute from wharf into export steamer.

Figure 22.2 Photographer unknown, 'Loading jute from wharf into export steamer', Calcutta, c.1900, photograph, 18.6 x 13.7 cm. Photo: Dundee University Archive Services

EXERCISE

Anthology Document 6.5, 'Booms and slumps in the Dundee textile industry', is an extract from a book by Alexander Warden about industry in Dundee written during the first jute boom. Warden suggests some reasons for Dundee's success. Read the extract now and answer the following questions:

1   What great changes in the linen industry does he describe?

2   To what does he attribute the success of the industry?

Spend about 25 minutes on this exercise.

SPECIMEN ANSWER

1   Warden describes two important changes: the switch from handlooms to powerlooms and from flax to jute.

2   In a word: war. He describes two booms and an intervening slump. In the 1850s, the Crimean War brought great prosperity to Dundee, but it was followed by a crash in 1857. The American Civil War brought renewed prosperity. Warden makes it clear that in both wars Dundee supplied both sides, even though in the Crimean War Britain was one of the combatants (and indeed its opponent was Russia, the source of much of the flax). In the American Civil War, the demand for linen was stimulated by a shortage of cotton as the North tried to block exports of raw cotton from the South to Lancashire. Warden has some concerns about this dependence on war ('production was extended greatly beyond the legitimate wants of consumers'), but does not deny the benefits to the town.

DISCUSSION

We usually associate linen (which is made from flax) with fine textiles, but it was also used in coarse materials such as sailcloth and sacking, much in demand during wars. Traditionally, linen was the main textile industry in Scotland, particularly in Dundee and the surrounding counties which concentrated on coarser products. In Unit 18, you encountered the enormous social tensions created by the expansion and mechanisation of the textile industry. In every textile industry, spinning was the first process to be mechanised and this created a great demand for handloom weavers until powerloom weaving was perfected. The switch to powerloom weaving (as indeed the earlier switch to mill-spinning) came much later in linen than in cotton. Flax was not an easy fibre to work with and a great deal of experimentation was needed before the correct techniques were found. Successful adaptation was a combination of imitating machines seen elsewhere, careful observation and on-the-job adjustment (Miskell and Whatley, 1999, p. 183).

Dundee's background in flax was essential to the success of the jute industry. Dundee spinners were used to working with a tough, brittle fibre and were able to adapt machines and techniques. Dundee was also a centre of the whale industry and whale oil was found to be good for softening jute. The city had a long tradition of selling low-price, coarse textiles and knew what buyers would look for. Jute first appears to have been used in the 1830s when flax prices began to rise. However, its use really took off during the Crimean War when demand was high and the supply of flax was threatened (Gauldie, 1987). Once its advantages were discovered, its advance was irresistible. Although some manufacturers continued to spin flax, jute soon became the dominant fibre. The combination of technical expertise in machine spinning and weaving and a tough, cheap fibre gave Dundee jute a competitive advantage over any other producer, including the substantial handloom jute industry in Bengal.

In explaining the switch from flax to jute, I have so far concentrated on the qualities of the new fibre and of Dundee as a manufacturing centre. But the switch was also one from a crop that was mainly grown outside the British empire to one grown within it. Although flax had been grown in Scotland and was still grown in Ireland, most flax came from Europe and especially from Russia's Baltic provinces. Jute, on the other hand, came from Bengal, which had been a British colony since the 1750s. Did British rule in India make jute more attractive to Dundee?

One way to answer such questions is to compare the flax and jute trades. In terms of production and transport, there were many similarities. Jute, unlike many tropical products (such as West Indian sugar), was never a plantation crop. It was grown by peasants, known as *ryots*, working small plots of land in the wet plains of the Ganges delta. Jute growing and preparation was very labour intensive and peasant farming drawing on labour from all the family was unbeatably cheap. Flax was also labour intensive and was mostly cultivated by peasants working their own land. There were also parallels in the organisation of the trade. In both cases, trade inside the country was organised by local merchants. Scottish merchants bought the flax or jute in port cities such as Riga or Calcutta.

How about the state? Here, of course, there was an important difference: Russia was independent while India was a British colony. Yet, in the mid nineteenth century, the policies they followed were not dissimilar. Bengal had been a British colony for a century before it started exporting jute to Dundee, and, as Bayly emphasises, the needs of British industry were not the reason for its conquest (Bayly, 1989). Once the jute trade developed, however, the colonial government was happy to encourage it. The Russian state took much the same view. It needed pounds sterling to buy British manufactured goods and flax exports were a good way to earn them. Does this mean Russia should be regarded as part of Britain's 'informal empire'? The question reveals the ambiguity of the term. While it might fit a country such as Argentina, where British influence was dominant, it makes little sense when used on a country that was strong enough to resist British pressure. If Russia exported jute, it was because the Russian government saw this as advantageous. If this was no longer the case, it would change its policies. Russia's high import tariffs were a constant irritation to the British government.

EXERCISE

What do you conclude from this discussion? Can the switch from flax to jute be explained in terms of empire?

Spend about 10 minutes on this exercise.

DISCUSSION

I have not supplied a specimen answer here as this question allows for more than one answer. If you concluded that the evidence presented suggests that imperial rule in India did not help make jute a more attractive raw material, you would be quite justified. It is hard to show that Dundee merchants or manufacturers secured a direct benefit in this way.

However, perhaps (thinking back to Hobsbawm, Cain and Hopkins) you took a broader view. There was one respect in which empire did contribute to *both* the flax and the jute trade. The rapid growth of international trade in the nineteenth century was based on safe shipping lanes, exchangeable currencies, the enforcement of legal agreements and low trade barriers – in short, a world of trust. Britain's naval and commercial power contributed substantially to this. The mid nineteenth century was in many ways the golden age of free trade – sometimes, indeed, referred to as the first age of globalisation.

Competition from Calcutta

EXERCISE

Now turn to the *Visual Sources*, Plate 22.1, which charts imports of jute and other fibres. How much does this graph tell us about the development of the Dundee textile industry?

Spend about 10–15 minutes on this exercise.

SPECIMEN ANSWER

We need to be cautious in using this data. The graph charts how much raw jute, flax and two other commodities was 'retained for consumption'; not what industry used.

The graph reveals a dramatic increase in net jute imports from the 1850s on. In 1855, it stood at around 30,000 tons; 60 years later, in 1915, it peaked at just short of 300,000 tons. Two phases in this process can be identified. From the 1850s until around 1883, the curve is mostly upward, although there were two dips in the late 1860s and the mid-1870s. After 1883, there is more fluctuation and some of the ups and downs are quite dramatic. Between 1903 and 1904, for instance, net imports almost halved. Overall, however, there is little increase: imports in 1883 were not much below those for 1915.

The graph also shows that jute imports came increasingly to Dundee only. In the 1870s, up to 20 per cent was used elsewhere; later the gap between national consumption and Dundee's narrowed. When Dundee (and the surrounding towns that used Dundee as a port, such as Forfar and Blairgowrie) was described as having a monopoly of the British jute industry, this was almost literally the case.

Finally, the graph shows that Dundee continued to use around 25,000 tons a year of flax and other fibres throughout the period until 1914. Jute may have been the growth industry, but it did not drive out flax.

DISCUSSION

If you noted that the table shows imports and not production, well done. The figures are derived from import and export data collected by customs officials (similar figures were used in Unit 14). Production figures were not recorded so carefully. Historians must use what quantitative data is available even if it does not precisely match their interests.

It is worth pausing to consider if there are reasons why import figures might not equal use in industry. Some jute imported to Britain was immediately re-exported for processing elsewhere, but this has been excluded from this table. A little was used for purposes other than textile manufacturing. More important was buying ahead. If prices fluctuated – and jute prices did – it might make sense to buy when it was cheap and store it for later. Such speculative buying was frequently condemned, which rather suggests it was common. However, although speculation might accentuate the peaks and troughs, it should not affect long-term trends: speculation only made sense if there were reasonable prospects that stocks would sell. Most raw jute imported to the UK was processed in Dundee, but despite dramatic fluctuations, imports ceased to grow after the mid-1880s.

EXERCISE

In view of these trends, it is perhaps not surprising that the heady optimism we encountered in the passage from Warden did not last. By the 1900s, the mood had changed, as Anthology Document 6.6, 'Summary of evidence presented to the Tariff Commission, 1905', reveals. Read it now and think about the problems faced by Dundee.

Spend just a few minutes on this exercise.

DISCUSSION

Dundee essentially faced two problems. First, as the passage describes, competitors, often using Dundee know-how, arose in other European countries and also in the United States. High tariffs, which pushed up the price of British goods, were often used to protect these industries. Dundee manufacturers also claimed that foreign manufacturers resorted to 'dumping', by which they meant selling in third countries at below the cost of production. They claimed that foreign manufacturers were able to do this because, behind their tariff barriers, they agreed on high fixed prices in their own countries (hence the reference to 'Kartells') and used the profits to subsidise sales elsewhere so as to capture the market.

The second problem is only hinted at in the text. Perhaps you noted the references to Calcutta. From the 1860s on, jute mills and factories were built on the Hooghly (Hughli) River, near Calcutta. Again, the machines and the men who set them up often came from Dundee. Once the industry was established in Calcutta, it enjoyed enormous advantages. Transport costs were cut – not only for the raw materials, which no longer needed to be shipped to Scotland, but Bengal was also closer to key markets such as the East Indies, Australia and Pacific North America. And labour was also much cheaper in Bengal. During the 1890s, Calcutta overtook Dundee; by 1914 it produced perhaps four times as much sacking (Stewart, 1998, pp. 2–3).

How could Dundee meet this threat? Throughout the late nineteenth century, Britain had resolutely stuck with its policy of free trade, but in 1903, Joseph Chamberlain (see p. 41 in Unit 21) raised the issue of tariff reform. He proposed that a system of imperial preference be introduced which would favour trade within the empire by imposing a tariff on imports from other countries. Ties between Britain and the colonies would be strengthened, revenue raised for spending on defence and social reform, and British markets protected for British manufacturers. Chamberlain's speech launched a national debate: rarely has an imperial issue played such a prominent role in British politics. For Cain and Hopkins, the defeat of tariff reform is one of the key victories of the City over industry (Cain and Hopkins, 1993, vol. 1, pp. 202–24).

EXERCISE

In Dundee, the national debate was contested in local terms. Anthology Document 6.7, 'The protectionist revival: letters by Dundee merchants', includes three extracts from correspondence in the local newspaper and one from a debate in the chamber of commerce. Read them now and consider the following questions:

1   What answers to overseas competition do the four writers see?

2   What comments do they have on the proposals made by others?

3   How do they view the relationship between 'home' and colony?

I have given you a fuller specimen answer than I would expect you to provide, but do go back to the documents as you read my answers to see for yourself how I have arrived at them.

Spend about 1 hour on this exercise.

SPECIMEN ANSWER

1   In letter (a), Victor Fraenkl focuses on foreign competition. His solution is an ingenious one: an export tax on all raw jute exported from the British empire. He argues that jute was effectively an imperial monopoly and Britain should exploit it. An export duty would force up the price of jute products made elsewhere thus making them less competitive (he in fact hoped that the threat of such a tax would force competitors to negotiate tariff reductions).

George Thom (letter b) is more concerned by the Calcutta industry and, in particular, by what he sees as the 'unfair' advantage of the lower standards required by the Indian Factory Acts.

If (a) and (b) suggest legislative changes, letter (c) argues that Dundee's salvation lies in concentrating on those areas where it still possesses competitive advantage. In his final paragraph, the writer points to a number of ways in which Dundee was still more competitive than Calcutta.

The final passage (d) is from a speech by John Leng, MP for Dundee (and also the editor of the *Advertiser*). Surely, rather a brave speech for the local MP to make! Leng's vision is an austere one and pure free-trade economics. Dundee once led in jute, but had now lost its advantage to Calcutta. There is no point in regrets – Dundee should move on. 'One trade rises and another decays.'

2   Two proposals for reform are made: an export tax on raw jute and reform of Indian factory legislation. Both draw comment – the writers did not mince their words! Thom (b) argues that an export tax will not help against Dundee's biggest competitor, Calcutta. Furthermore, both (b) and (c) highlight the risk of retaliation. Jute manufacturers in both Dundee and Calcutta wanted to export jute, not protect their home markets. They had a lot to lose in a tariff war; furthermore, Calcutta had nothing to gain. Jute manufacture in Calcutta was so cheap that it was competitive in most markets, even some of those with tariffs. At this stage in their history, they were as confident of their ability to compete as Dundee had been 40 years before. 'A Calcutta Dundonian' (c) has a cutting phrase about '50 or 60 manufacturers in a Scotch town'.

The idea that a tougher Factory Act in India would benefit Dundee is also dismissed in (c). It argues that conditions for 'women and children' are better in Calcutta anyway (this is a clever debating point, as we shall see later in the unit). Furthermore, if factory hours were equalised, it would do little to diminish the difference in production costs. (Leng would probably have agreed. He wrote a report on a visit to Calcutta, which was very complimentary about factory conditions.)

3   So far, we have focused on their arguments. The last question asks about the underlying assumptions. Phrases in (a) and (d) suggest rather different ideas of the relationship. Fraenkl's position is perhaps the most straightforward. India is a British colony – it should be used to benefit Britain (and, in this case, Dundee). Leng takes almost the opposite position; 'the Mother Country' has duties towards its dependencies. His language suggests a parental relationship, but one which involves duties on the part of the parent. What of the other two? Thom also uses family images ('the children of our own household'), but India here is not a dutiful child worthy of protection but a cuckoo in the nest. In this text, India is a threat – a surprising way of looking at a colony! Finally, our 'Calcutta Dundonian' – can he be read as a champion of India? The title he has chosen makes clear that he is a Scot. If India deserves fair treatment, the equality he seeks is for expatriate businessmen. This is the empire not as a market for British goods but as a field in which Britons (or Scots) might make good.

The advocates of protection won the debate in the Dundee chamber of commerce by 92 votes to 45. But in the nation as a whole, tariff reform was less successful. In the 1906 election, the Liberal party made great play of the cost of tariffs ('a tax on bread') and won by a landslide.

In fact, there was never much chance that tariffs would be manipulated to benefit Dundee. Some of the weaknesses of the case for protection have already been identified. Tariffs may help to protect a home market, but jute, like many British industries, was export oriented. Imposing British tariffs risked retaliation, which would harm Britain – the world's greatest exporter. Moreover, Dundee's main competitor was inside the British empire. Chamberlain's proposals were supposed to bring the empire together, but many in the dominions were anxious to protect their fledgling industries. The leaders of the tariff reform movement could not afford to be associated with proposals, such as those emanating from Dundee, where imperial rule was to be exploited for Britain's benefit. Furthermore, in contrast, say, to the Lancashire cotton industry, Dundee was just too small to count on the national stage. Whereas Lancashire had 60 MPs in the House of Commons, Dundee had just two. Moreover, their rivals in Calcutta were closer to power. The Bombay cotton manufacturers who challenged Lancashire were mostly Indian; all the jute mills on the Hooghly were still owned and managed by British expatriate firms and the jute 'wallahs' of Calcutta had far better connections in London and New Delhi than Dundee did (Stewart, 1998, pp. 10–2).

There is another reason why the British government was unlikely to do anything that would limit the Calcutta jute industry. By the end of the nineteenth century, with the rise of the American and German economies,

Britain's trade deficit was growing rapidly.[1] As rising tariffs excluded British goods from foreign markets, imperial markets became more important and, among these, India was one of the largest. India in turn, had a trade surplus with the USA, and raw and manufactured jute were important exports. There was thus a trade triangle between the three countries that helped maintain Britain's trading position and so made Britain, as London was well aware, dependant on Calcutta's export performance (Sethia, 1996, pp. 94–8).

Summary

This section has looked at the rise of the Dundee jute industry and its subsequent difficulties. Overseas links have been emphasised: the raw material came from India and markets were global. Yet, the benefits of empire to Dundee remain hard to define. There is little to suggest that the switch to jute was facilitated by British rule in Bengal and imperial government was not used to protect Dundee's staple.

THE ORGANISATION OF THE JUTE INDUSTRY

Firms and competition

So far, we have discussed the jute industry as a whole. But any industry is composed of enterprises. Further insights into Dundee's links to empire can be gained from taking the case study approach a stage further and looking at how individual firms adapted to the demands of an industry based on global networks.

The following is a description of the jute and linen 'market' in Dundee:

> Almost all the day to day business was carried on between merchants and manufacturers in a 'market' shelter which had been built next to the Chamber of Commerce building about 1889. In fine weather this overflowed into Panmure Street outside, regardless of the effect this might have on the passing traffic. Contracts were all verbal, to be confirmed later in writing, and this system worked well until 1939 when it ceased on the outbreak of war in that year. Markets were held daily (Monday to Friday) between the hours of 3 pm and 4 pm and one could usually tell on arrival from the hum of conversation whether business was active or the reverse.
>
> (Halley, 1980, p. 20)

---

[1] The deficit was a trade deficit only: Britain imported more goods than it exported. However, Britain also earned money abroad on 'invisible exports' (such as insurance) and enjoyed considerable revenues from investments overseas. Added together, these sources of revenue left Britain with a healthy surplus overall, but the trade deficit was a source of concern in a country that had long prided itself on being 'the workshop of the world'.

The writer was born in 1900 and took over the running of his family firm, William Halley & Sons Ltd, in 1925, and so his memories are likely to be of the market as it was in the interwar years rather than earlier. Nevertheless, his description tallies with what we know for earlier periods. Figure 22.3 shows Panmure Street and one can see a crowd of businessmen, many in bowlers, behind the park railings. Although the photo caption provides few details, it seems likely that this was the market in action. The 'market shelter' (a more solid building than the word 'shelter' might suggest) can be seen in the background.

What was going on? Halley talks of 'merchants and manufacturers'. In 1900, the *Dundee Directory* lists fifteen shipping companies, fifty-four brokers, fifty-four commission agents, and over 150 merchants. The jute trade was one with many participants. From the peasant producers in Bengal, to the buyers of jute sacks in Argentina or the Mid-West, jute passed through many hands. At each stage – transportation to Calcutta, compressing the bales, shipping to Dundee, spinning, weaving, preparing the cloth for sale, and selling overseas – there were many competing firms offering the same service. William Lazonick contrasts Britain's nineteenth-century 'market-coordinated industrial economy' with American managerial capitalism in the twentieth century. Nineteenth-century British firms, he argues, were specialists who relied on external networks for supplies and marketing (Lazonick, 1991). Most Dundee enterprises only engaged in one part of the process of jute trading and production – relying on the market for supplies (in the case of a spinner, raw jute) and sales (yarn). Hence the importance of the Panmure Street market.

EXERCISE

Warden's book includes a list of textile manufacturers in Dundee in 1864. You will find this in Anthology Document 6.8, 'Textile manufacturers in Dundee, 1864'. Examine it now and consider the following questions:

1   What does this list tell you about the scale and structure of the industry?

2   What does it tell you about the manufacturers?

Spend about 15–20 minutes on this exercise.

SPECIMEN ANSWER

1   Sixty-one companies engaged in the same industry is a large number for a small area; all the firms listed had their factories within three miles of the town centre. Some of the firms are very large. Using the number of employees ('hands' as Warden terms them), nine firms are listed as having 1,000 workers or over, with the largest (Baxter Brothers & Co.) employing 4,000 – a large workforce in any period. However, there are also many smaller ones – there are twenty-four firms with 200 workers or fewer.

The columns headed 'Spindles' and 'Power looms' denote the two major branches of the industry: spinning and weaving. Some of the firms are engaged in both – thus Baxter Brothers has 19,744 spindles and 1,200 looms. But many of the smaller firms, and one or two of the larger ones, were only involved in one part of the process. O. G. Miller, for instance, has the third largest number of spindles but no looms. Most of the very smallest firms were only engaged in weaving. Firms that only spun or wove would, of course, need to sell or buy yarn.

Figure 22.3 Alexander Wilson, Panmure Street, Dundee, 1900, from original glass negative. Photo: Dundee City Council, Central Library. Note the crowd in front of the Royal Exchange (home of the Chamber of Commerce) behind the park railings. The 'market shelter' is the building to the left of the Exchange.

2   There is not a lot to go on here. However, the names of the firms are interesting
    – every name on the list is that of one or more individuals. In many cases, the
    name suggests that the firm was owned by a single individual or by a family –
    brothers or a father and son. In other cases, the name suggests a partnership
    between unrelated individuals. None of the firms have 'Ltd' after their names.

DISCUSSION

It is possible that not all the firms were owned by one or a few individuals and that
the names disguise more complex ownerships patterns. However, legislation
allowing limited liability had only existed since 1856 and was long not widely used.
It is therefore very likely that all the firms were unincorporated, which would mean
that the owners or partners were fully liable for the debts of their firms. Under such
circumstances, trust was important, and this often meant that businessmen
preferred to enter partnerships with closely related individuals.

Warden wrote his book at a time of great change and it is perhaps not
surprising that there were so many textile firms in Dundee in this period: many
may have been keen to try their luck in the boom industry. Powerlooms were
also new in 1864. It is often the case that barriers to entry are low in a time of
rapid technological change – think of the dot.com boom at the turn of the
twenty-first century. Many of the smallest firms in Warden's table were only
weavers and it seems likely that the new technology was seen by new men as
an opportunity to make their fortune. But the dot.com boom was followed by a
slump and many of the new firms failed. What happened in Dundee when
conditions got tougher?

Frustratingly, I was not able to trace a comparable list for a later period. In
general, firms were regarded as the private property of their owners in
nineteenth-century Britain and, as a result, we have rather less information on
British businesses than is the case for many other countries (including,
interestingly, India). So I used the valuation rolls (a list of property for local
taxation) for an industrial ward in the city to explore which textile companies
were there in 1864, 1880 and 1900. Table 22.1 summarises what I found.

Table 22.1   Textile firms in Ward 8, Burgh of Dundee

	1864	1880	1900
Firms there in 1864	20	14	8
New in 1880		9	2
New in 1900			12
Total	20	23	22

(Source: Valuation rolls for the Burgh of Dundee (ward boundaries as in 1900))

The table shows no reduction in the total number of firms. Only eight of the
firms survived throughout the period, but as some firms dropped out, others
replaced them. This continued to happen after 1880, even though, by then, the

boom conditions of the 1860s and 1870s had passed. Interestingly, more of the firms that had survived 1864–1880 survived to 1900 than did new ones.

If the value of the property can be taken as a measure of the size of the firm, then the largest firm in 1864 was still the largest in 1900. But the second and third largest in 1864 (no. 2 was O. G. Miller) had disappeared by 1900. The survivors in 1900 included some that had been quite small in 1864, and, although most had higher valuations in 1900 than in 1864, many were still in the middle ranks of the table. If most new entrants started small, some were able to start big by taking over factories. The failure of O. G. Miller in 1884 put its five mills on the market and these were taken over by other firms, including some newcomers.

These patterns – high exit and entry rates, the survival of the biggest firms but also of many smaller ones, business failures creating opportunities for new men – appear to have been true of Dundee as a whole. There was no consolidation in the industry by merger and takeover (as was to happen in the even tougher trading conditions after the First World War).

A high-risk trade

EXERCISE

Why was there so much turnover in the stock of companies? You will recall the peaks and troughs in Plate 22.1. Anthology Document 6.9, 'The Dundee local trade in 1892', is a look back on a year that included one of the downturns; read the document now. What happened in 1892?

Spend about 30 minutes on this exercise.

SPECIMEN ANSWER

In the early part of the year, fears concerning the supply of raw jute from Bengal pushed up prices; this was made worse by a 'bull market' in which every rumour raised expectations – and prices – further. When more accurate information about the size of the jute crop reached Dundee, it became clear that there would be plenty of jute available and prices fell. The whole process was made worse, in the opinion of the writer, by speculation: the buying and selling of raw jute, not for manufacture, but because it was hoped that a profit could be made on trading.

DISCUSSION

This is not an easy text to follow and this is, in itself, interesting. It was obviously felt that readers would have a certain understanding of local markets. The passage brings out two important constraints on the jute industry. First, raw jute was an agricultural commodity and supply depended on harvests. The fact that nearly all jute was produced in just one region of the world, and one subject to extreme weather conditions, meant that the supply could vary dramatically from year to year. Secondly, the nature of the trade meant that information was often poor. With so many peasant producers, it was difficult to find out in advance how good the harvest would be. The distances involved, and the number of market participants, meant that rumours abounded and could not easily be checked. The result was 'violent fluctuations' and 'rash speculation'. At one point in 1892, prices fell so far that it was not worth shipping jute and supplies threatened to dry up. Buying and selling at the right price often made the difference between success and failure. Looking back on the interwar years, a businessman could recall:

> Going each day to the market at the Merchant's Shelter and attempting to buy yarn one ninety-sixth of a penny cheaper than it was offered because efficiency of production hardly affected profits – all depended on the price of the raw material.
>
> (Quoted in Gauldie, 1987, p. 114)

These were tough conditions for manufacturers, and the risks were high. Remember that partners in an unincorporated partnership were fully liable for the debts of their firm. You might expect that entrepreneurs would be cautious about entering such an industry and that many firms would fail. Yet, as we have seen, there continued to be new entrants into the jute industry and some firms, including small ones, survived. In the following example we will explore how this was achieved.

Harry Walker & Sons Ltd

Harry Walker & Sons, jute spinners and manufacturers, was founded in 1873 by Harry Walker, after he had split up with his brother (J. & H. Walker is no. 60 in Warden's 1864 list). A modern factory, the Caldrum works, was built (see Figure 22.4). The firm became a limited company in 1892 with a paid-up capital of £150,000, divided between 10,000 £10 ordinary shares and 5,000 £10 preference shares (if you are unsure of the precise meaning of these terms, check the glossary). The directors were Harry Walker, his sons, and later his grandsons, and they and their spouses and daughters held virtually all the shares.

Among the business records that have survived, the most informative are probably the balance sheets and annual reports for the period after incorporation. Balance sheets need to be seen as a primary source like any other: the same questions about authorship, purpose and audience are relevant. In the case of a company like Harry Walker & Sons, with no outside shareholders, such questions throw up some interesting answers: the 'authors' (officially, the directors) and the 'audience' (the shareholders) were virtually the same. Although accounts had to be audited, in this period there was no requirement to publish them. In the case of Harry Walker & Sons, the balance sheets that have been preserved are handwritten and amendments have been made on the documents. They give every appearance of being for use within the firm only. The balance sheets of public companies in this period were notoriously unreliable, but, in a privately owned firm such as this one, there were few advantages to be gained from concealing results (Arnold, 1995). We can perhaps see them as the directors' own assessment of their situation.

Figure 22.4 Photographer unknown, Workers (including women in shawls) leaving Caldrum Works, Dundee, *c*.1900, photograph, 25 x 20 cm. Photo: Courtesy of University of Dundee Archive Services

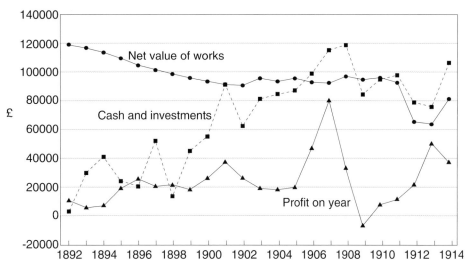

Figure 22.5 Harry Walker & Sons Ltd: profits, value of works and investments, 1892–1914.
Source: based on company records from Dundee University Archive, MS66/VI/7/1

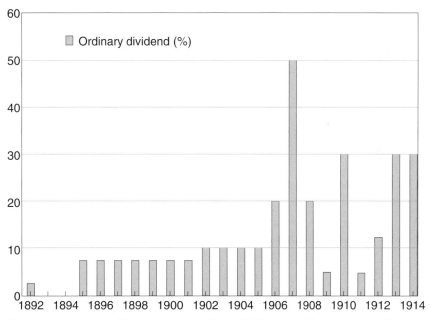

Figure 22.6 Harry Walker & Sons Ltd: ordinary dividends, 1892–1914. Source: based on
company records from Dundee University Archive, MS66/VI/7/1

EXERCISE

Figures 22.5 and 22.6 are charts based on figures from the balance sheets and
annual reports.

1   Do the charts suggest that Harry Walker & Sons was profitable?

2   What happened to the value of the works, as compared with 'cash and
     investments'?

3   What do the charts suggest was done with the profits?

Spend about 20–25 minutes on this exercise.

SPECIMEN ANSWER

1   Yes, Figure 22.5 shows that profits were made in every year except 1909; 1907 and 1913 were particularly good years.

2   The value of the works declined gently until around 1900 and were then roughly stable until a big drop in 1912. The value of cash and investments, on the other hand, rose irregularly to around 1908. By 1914, they had exceeded the value of the works for seven of the last nine years. A curious inversion for a manufacturing company!

3   Figure 22.6 shows the amount the company paid out to ordinary shareholders. From 1895 to 1905, ordinary dividends were held steady at 7.5 per cent and later 10 per cent. (10 per cent dividends meant that the company paid out 10 per cent of the face value of the ordinary shares, i.e. £1 per share). As we know from Figure 22.5, this was a period when 'cash and investments' were rising. The figures suggest that not all profits were paid out and money was kept in the firm for the first 15 years. After 1906, policy seems to have changed. Higher dividends were paid, transferring profits from the firm to the family.

DISCUSSION

We do need to treat the figures with caution. In particular, too little allowance was probably made for depreciation in the value of the works. It is possible that concerns about this led to the big drop in 1912, when £25,226 was suddenly written off. The figures also do not tell us what turnover was required to generate these profits, but there can be no doubt that Harry Walker & Sons was profitable. When things were going well, big profits were made and even in years of crisis, such as 1892 (remember Anthology Document 6.9), they still broke even. From 1895 on, despite the ups and downs of the jute industry, they never missed a dividend.

How did they do it? The balance sheets and the annual reports suggest a number of factors:

• They were good at holding down costs. The annual reports in the 1890s often report short-time working and machines kept idle. When demand was slack, they reduced the hours worked and their wages bill. As Figure 22.5 shows, in most years more was written off the value of the works than was invested in them. With little investment and few debts, they could afford to sit out downturns in the trade.

• They held large and fluctuating stocks of jute. We already know that good buying was essential to success. The company's large cash reserves mean that it could afford to buy when prices were good and hold stocks. The figures in their balance sheets suggest they held, on average, 8,000 tons of jute – 45,000 of the bales in Figure 22.7 – in the years between 1892 and 1914. Interestingly, the only loss followed a decision to write down stocks – presumably following a wrong guess on price movements.

• Since all the shareholders were family, pressure to pass on profits through high dividends may have been less. Directors could choose to hold profits in the firm, or, as after 1906, transfer them to the family.

Figure 22.7   Photographer unknown, Jute on horse drays at Victoria Spinning Co. Ltd., 1920s, photograph, 19.9 x 15.1 cm. Photo: Courtesy of University of Dundee Archive Services. Each bale weighed around 400 lbs

Summary and implications

Consider what we have learnt about the structure of the Dundee jute industry. It was composed of many firms, most of them carrying out only one part of the process of buying, transporting, manufacturing and selling jute. New entrants gave the industry dynamism: they saw opportunities and took risks that might well end in disaster. Harry Walker may have started in this way, but by the 1890s the firm was no longer taking big risks. Reserves gave the firm resilience; experience of a highly competitive and volatile industry made it cautious. One might describe their strategy as prioritising survival (and waiting for opportunities – in 1914, the First World War broke out and the demand for sandbags soared).

Bruce Lenman and Kathleen Donaldson have suggested that the legacy of the jute industry was disastrous for Dundee. Big profits were made in jute, but these were invested overseas rather than in the local economy (there is a parallel to Hobson's 'surplus capital' argument in Anthology Document 6.1). From the 1870s on, investment trusts launched by Dundee businessmen channelled enormous sums into foreign investments and particularly into American railway, land and cattle companies. Dundee's 'jute barons' preferred to invest in American stocks rather than in developing new industries in Dundee. The result left Dundee dangerously dependent on an industry in trouble (Lenman and Donaldson, 1971).

Interestingly, some of Harry Walker & Sons' capital was held in American trust funds, which would have given a return of around 6 per cent. This suggests that the directors saw this as a better return (or at least a safer investment) than could be obtained at home. In this they were not alone: the wills of Dundee businessmen often reveal large overseas investments. And Britain as a whole between the 1870s and the First World War, invested heavily abroad, in the empire (particularly Canada, South Africa and Australasia), but also in Latin America and, above all, the USA. One-fifth of all overseas investment in 1865–1914 went to the USA alone. On the whole, economic historians have calculated that this was of benefit to Britain – the return on investments overseas was higher than could have been obtained in the UK (Edelstein, 2004, p. 194). What of Harry Walker & Sons? Could they have invested more in Dundee? Remember how narrow was their business experience. The complicated networks built up to bring jute from Bengal, manufacture it, and sell the products to markets all over the world could not easily be switched to a new industry. Dundee did jute. For business families like the Walkers, the choice was jute or a safe investment overseas.

PICTURING DUNDEE

Maps and photographs

So far, the focus has been on the development and the organisation of the jute industry. The next section turns to how Dundee was shaped by the industry, and in particular to a number of contemporary views of the city. For this, a range of sources are available, including non-textual ones. Earlier blocks have explored how visual sources can be used to understand past societies. By the nineteenth century, photography provides a new medium.

EXERCISE

To start with, however, read Anthology Document 6.10, 'A tourist description of Dundee', and look at Plate 22.2 in the *Visual Sources*. Anthology Document 6.10 is a brief description of Dundee from *Murray's Handbook for Scotland*, the sort of guidebook a tourist might have taken on a visit to Scotland. Obviously, most of this guide is devoted to tourist areas (Loch Lomond and the Trossachs are well covered), but Dundee is also described. The map in Plate 22.2 is also taken from the *Handbook*.

Spend just a few minutes on this exercise.

Anthology Document 6.10 highlights the way that Dundee was perceived by contemporaries: as a centre of industry, dominated by jute. The map helps us understand this perception. At the foot of the plan, the docks and railways dominate the waterfront: the early nineteenth-century harbour near the town centre (Earl Grey and King William IV docks) had been extended eastward with new docks and wharves in the 1860s and 1870s. The plan names many works (such as the Caldrum and Manhattan works near the top of the map, and the Ward and Tay works to the west of the centre). The area west of the Tay works was also largely industrial, and many of the streets between the harbour and Seagate were lined with warehouses. In nearly all parts of the city, factories and housing were mixed – note, for instance, how close the houses with gardens north of Victoria Road are to the Dens and Wallace works. Such houses were middle-class islands in what was a predominantly working-class town centre. The grey blocks between most of the streets contained tenements, the three- or four-storey buildings of flats that were the standard housing in urban Scotland. Several of the public buildings and spaces in the city – such as the Baxter Park in the east – were named after their industrial benefactors. Just before the First World War, Dundee acquired a new town hall, the Caird Hall, named after another textile baron. In Dundee, jute was inescapable.

EXERCISE

Turning now to some early photographs of the city, look at Plates 22.3 and 22.4 in the *Visual Sources*. These were both taken by Alexander Wilson in 1888.

What do these photographs tell us about Dundee? As with other images, think also about how they are composed.

Spend about 15 minutes on this exercise.

SPECIMEN ANSWER

The ships in both photos are clearly cargo vessels and are moored in front of warehouses. It is striking that there were so many sailing ships still in use; by the 1880s one would expect steamships, like the *Loch Garry*, to be more common. One imagines that they were bringing the flax and jute on which Dundee's industry depended. Both photos show the tall chimneys of a factory town; there are at least eight in the second photo, although the murk, probably itself the result of the chimneys, makes it difficult to see.

The lines are perhaps the most striking compositional feature. In Plate 22.3, the lines of the mastheads, the horizon, and the ships' hulls lead towards the main activity in the picture – the ship that is raising or lowering its sails. In Plate 22.4, the roof of the warehouse cuts straight across the photo, dividing the city from the harbour. This might have the effect of cutting the view in two, but certainly does bring out the sleek lines of the steamship. Both photos are also surprisingly quiet for harbour scenes, with almost no people to be seen.

DISCUSSION

Such effects were not accidental: we can assume that Alexander Wilson organised these photos carefully. The stillness of the photos was not a result of the methods used: by the 1880s, a photo could be taken in seconds. If there are few people in the photos it is because Wilson chose to photograph the harbour so as to avoid activity. Although we know relatively little about Alexander Wilson, his interests and style suggest that he was influenced by the Record and Survey Movement of the 1880s, which set out to faithfully photograph images such as buildings about to be demolished or vanishing handcrafts. 'Five ships in Dundee Docks' is far more likely to be the result of a desire to capture a disappearing age than to show a working harbour.

Flax and jute continued to be transported by sail longer than most goods since they were bulky, low-price and non-perishable commodities. Nevertheless, by the early 1890s, this was changing. In 1885, fifty-eight jute ships from Calcutta docked at Dundee, of which only seven were steamships; by 1892, of the forty-one Calcutta ships, twenty-five were steam. The steamships carried more and were faster; after 1901, there were virtually no sailing ships left on this route. Wilson's collection contains hundreds of photos of sailing ships, but relatively few of steamships. We do not know whether Wilson sold these particular photos, but he did work for Valentine's, one of Scotland's largest producers of the picture postcards that were so popular at the turn of the century. Such postcards often featured the old-fashioned and 'quaint'.

There is always a temptation with old photographs to assume that they will simply reveal how the past looked, and it is important to ask the same questions as for other primary sources. They were created according to artistic conventions and with specific purposes in mind. These conventions operate like scaffolding. They provide necessary support during construction but are no longer visible in the finished work. Although Wilson photographed an actual scene, his choice of framing (what to include or exclude), lighting (light and shade determine mood) and timing allowed him to impose his interpretation on what we see.

Bearing this in mind, please look at the photos of Dundee in the *Visual Sources*, Plates 22.5 and 22.6. These are taken from *The Photographic Survey* made by the Dundee and East of Scotland Photographic Society and supported by the town council. According to a report in the *Dundee Yearbook*:

> The purpose is to have for preservation in the Dundee Museum a vast collection of photographs of Dundee at the present day. While antique buildings that still survive will be duly chronicled, modern structures that show the style of the time, churches, public buildings, streets, and all that exhibits the social life of the early twentieth century will be included.
>
> ('The Photographic Survey', *Dundee Yearbook*, 1905, p. 122)

There are a number of points I would like you to focus on in these photographs:

- Plate 22.5 shows the Camperdown jute works in Lochee. The text that accompanies the photograph explains that the works covered 30 acres and employed almost 5,000 (*Murray's Guide* listed the same facts!). 'Built upon a definite plan, throughout they present uniformity of design and harmony in detail. Each department is equipped with the most up-to-date appliances, and all details involved in the technique of manufacture receive scrupulous attention. The photograph contains a fair reflex of these extensive works' (*Photographic Survey*, p. 11).

- The way the photograph has been taken serves to accentuate this emphasis on size and function. The ornate clock tower on the spinning mill may be in the centre of the photo, but the dominant impression is of the functional loom sheds to its right and storehouses to its left. The clock itself emphasises the importance of time in an industrial age. The photo must have been taken from the 282 foot chimney, Cox's Stack, which dominates the site and is still standing today.

- This photo might be contrasted with Plate 22.6 of Baxter Brothers' Dens works, also from *The Photographic Survey*. Dens works were much closer to the town centre and the buildings are crowded together. With less space to expand, the mills were built higher. Here too, however, they are functional and largely unornamented – it is hard to distinguish the mills in the foreground from the tenements in the back left.

- Neither photo includes people, which must have required careful planning in the case of Plate 22.5. This is indeed true of virtually all the photos of works in the *Survey* collection. This, and the way sky is largely excluded by the angle chosen, serves to create a grimly utilitarian impression.

Some of the other photos in this unit are from the records of Dundee jute and flax firms. We do not know exactly why such photos were collected, but it seems probable that the companies wanted them either as a record or for publicity purposes. In these cases too, even if we cannot always know answers, we need to think about composition and purpose when considering what such sources tell us about contemporary perceptions of Dundee.

A 'women's town'

Figures 22.8 and 22.9 bring out another side of Dundee at the end of the century: its appalling poverty. The following quotation is Wentworth D'Arcy Thomson, appointed professor at Dundee's new University College in 1884, recalling, fifty years later, his first impressions of the city:

> Dundee was terribly poor. When I first came here the Greenmarket was full of idle men, walking to and fro, hungry and in rags. Of all those young professors who had come to Town, I doubt if there was not one who was not shocked and saddened by the poverty which Dundee openly displayed ... Dundee was worse even than the slums of London, Glasgow, and Liverpool.
>
> (Quoted in Lenman and Donaldson, 1971, p. 18)

D'Arcy Thomson went on to become one of the founders of the Dundee Social Union, a middle-class organisation that campaigned for reform. One of their great achievements was a widely read report on poverty in the city.

EXERCISE

Read the extract from the report in Anthology Document 6.11, 'Report of the committee of the Dundee Social Union', and answer the following questions:

1   How would you describe the tone of this document? Why do you think this tone was chosen?

2   What do the writers see as the main cause of the city's problems?

3   What link do they make in their final two paragraphs?

Spend about 30 minutes on this exercise.

SPECIMEN ANSWER

1   The tone is resolutely objective. The authors are keen to present their findings as research led and not driven by emotions (although they let their views show in the final sentence of the first paragraph). As they explain, they hope to persuade 'public opinion' to address the problems they have identified; they evidently believe this tone is the most likely to succeed.

2   No attempt is made to challenge the economic maxims of the day. To compete with India, labour must be cheap: this is 'beyond the control of the employers'. Accepted, too, is that cheap labour means female labour. This is, however, the main reason for the city's poverty. According to the report, nothing would help Dundee more than more work for men.

3   In the final paragraphs, the report links the employment of women to the health of children. Figures for infant mortality are highlighted.

DISCUSSION

In highlighting health, the Dundee Social Union was choosing its arguments carefully. There was great concern about the 'condition of the people' following the Boer War, when it had been discovered that many volunteers were unfit for military duty. By linking poverty to infant mortality and 'weedy, unhealthy men and women', the Dundee Social Union hoped to capitalise on this mood. In focusing on women workers, the writers were drawing attention to one of the most striking facts about labour in Dundee. According to their estimates, 73 per cent of labour in the jute industry was female (and only 16 per cent adult men) (Dundee Social Union, 1905, p. 48). Wages were notoriously low, and employment uncertain – you will recall that

Figure 22.8 Alexander Wilson, Hawkhill, Dundee, c.1895, photograph from original glass negative. Photo: Dundee City Council, Central Library

Figure 22.9 Alexander Wilson, Perth Road, Dundee, c.1895, photograph from original glass negative. Photo: Dundee City Council, Central Library

Harry Walker & Sons laid off employees when business was slow. The emphasis here, however, is on women as mothers: for married women to go out to work was considered 'unnatural'. Here too the Dundee Social Union was drawing on accepted conventions: while it was still widely held that the state had no role in relations between employers and male employees, the need to step in and protect female and child workers had long been established.

A consequence of this approach was that the female workers of Dundee's jute mills (see Figure 22.10) were seen as victims. This view was for long also adopted by historians. The weakness of trade unions among Dundee's women textile workers led many to conclude that they were too downtrodden and apathetic to organise properly. Eleanor Gordon, however, suggests an alternative interpretation. Between 1889 and 1914, she traced 103 strikes involving women jute workers in Dundee (Gordon, 1991, p. 190). Most involved just one firm, although a few spread across town, involving up to 35,000 workers. Most were spontaneous and were launched by the workers themselves rather than called by unions. News spread by word of mouth, supported by pickets at the entrance to the works (see Figure 22.4), 'symbolic sites for both employers and employees, as the only point of entry and exit' (Wainwright, 2005, p. 133). The following two extracts from the *Dundee Advertiser* (no friend of the strikers!) gives a flavour of how strikes might progress.

> At Tay works, the great spinning and weaving establishments of Messrs Gilroy Sons and Company, there was also a gathering of malcontents who 'demonstrated' according to the accepted fashion. The general body of hands seemed undecided, but most of them in the end filed past the porter's lodge. At the dinner hour, however, evidently impressed by the knowledge of what was going on elsewhere, their ranks were largely augmented.
> (*Dundee Advertiser*, 24 February 1906, quoted in Gordon, 1991, p. 205)

> Strikers invaded the Cowgate ... 'in a twinkling', a circle, the diameter of which extended from the Queen's Statue to the portals of the shelter was formed, and a couple of score of shrieking, shouting spinners spun round in the gyrations of jingo ring ... ere long Panmure Street was thronged from end to end by an uproarious crowd of lassies. Number gave them boldness and they made a rush for the shelter, in which for the most part millowners seeking to escape personal allusion and recognition had taken refuge ... A hooting band made a rush for the last door, but the police, who acted with commendable discretion intervened and the portals were closed.
> (*Dundee Advertiser*, 27 February 1906, quoted in Gordon, 1991, p. 208)

Spontaneous action, Gordon argues, 'maximized disruption by being unpredictable and, as a display of united action, could also serve to heighten the self-respect and self-regard of the women'; the public ridicule of the millowners 'challenged patriarchal authority' (pp. 206, 208). Such strikes were

Figure 22.10 Photographer unknown, Women weavers at their looms inside Dens Works, c.1908, photograph, 20 x 25 cm. Photo: Courtesy of University of Dundee Archive Services

usually short-lived because the women's low wages would not allow them to sustain a long strike, but this did not mean they were necessarily ineffective. Success depended on stopping one mill (when the others continued working) or bringing the town to a standstill. In such a competitive industry, firms could not afford to stand idle when demand was high. If demand was slow, however, firms such as Harry Walker & Sons were quite happy to sit strikes out. Success depended on the state of the market – as did so much else in Dundee.

Summary

In this section, we have looked at some of the ways contemporaries perceived Dundee. One striking feature is the importance of production in these perceptions. The tourist guide, the photos, and the Dundee Social Union report on the city all highlight aspects of the process of production. When pickets blocked factory gates, or mill girls mobbed manufacturers, they were drawing on identities defined by their role in the manufacture of jute.

CONCLUSION

EXERCISE

Before starting on the case study of Dundee, I asked you to keep a note of points where you felt the Cain and Hopkins thesis provided insights or raised questions. I would now like you to reflect on your notes. You may find it helpful to look back at the discussion of Cain and Hopkins.

Spend about 30 minutes on this exercise.

DISCUSSION

There are many points that could be made and I will not attempt to provide a specimen answer. But perhaps you will have come up with some of the following (the numbers and letters refer to the points given in specimen answers on pp. 50–2):

- Although this unit has focused on just one industry, we have seen how the ramifications of the global jute trade reached into every aspect of Dundee life, from the ships in the harbour to relations between men and women. Business success or failure or the wages paid to employees could be affected by events on the far side of the globe. To study Dundee without taking empire into account would indeed be absurd (1).

- We need, however, to consider what we mean by the term 'empire'. If only the territories ruled by Britain are meant, then only some of the overseas dimensions to Dundee's jute trade are captured. The industry was no respecter of imperial boundaries. Dundee did switch from Russian flax to Indian jute, but not because the latter came from within the empire. Markets were found all over the world. When jute is described as an imperial industry, we are following Cain and Hopkins (and Hobsbawm) in using the term empire to describe a global economic system dominated by Britain (2).

- You may, however, have been struck by how few tangible benefits the Dundee jute industry seems to have gained from the British empire. The term 'informal empire' does not really help us understand the Baltic flax trade. Nor, later, when Dundee's jute industry wanted help, did the British authorities in India manipulate trading conditions to favour Dundee (although they did aid Lancashire). To Dundonians, it seemed at times a distinct disadvantage that its main competitor was also within the empire. Admittedly, imperial and 'informal empire' markets offered Dundee merchants some protection when foreign countries put up tariffs to exclude Dundee goods. But this was a poor recompense for the more lucrative markets from which Dundee was excluded (2).

- Returning to Cain and Hopkins's thesis, we should perhaps not be surprised by this. The manufacturers of Dundee were certainly no 'gentlemen capitalists'! Cain and Hopkins argue that industry had little influence on government and this was certainly Dundee's experience. The discussion of tariff reform showed that Dundee counted for little in government circles (3).

- Tariff reform divided the city. As the texts we have studied reveal, the Dundee jute merchants and manufacturers certainly possessed a strong sense of communal identity. Yet, when it came to one of the key issues of the age, industry did not speak with one voice. Does this undermine the idea of a 'jute lobby' let alone an industry one? (3 and A).

- Dundee capitalists were investors as well as producers. However, I am not sure we should attach too much importance to this: the Walker family would certainly have seen themselves as industrialists. But note that their main investment destination was the USA. Again, business did not stop at imperial boundaries (3, A and a bit of 2).

- By the 1890s, the Dundee jute industry was on the defensive: the pattern of its trade fits more closely to Hobsbawm's 'retreat' into empire than Cain and Hopkins's image of Britain as a 'dynamic and ambitious power'. Yet in this Dundee was unusual: competition from what is now termed the 'Third World' affected jute before almost any other industry. What Dundee experienced in the 1890s would affect Lancashire cotton in the interwar years (4 and C).

- What of Cannadine's concern that 'gentlemanly capitalism' does not explain Scottish participation in empire? There is little in this unit that supports this concern. Indeed, I found Marshall more enlightening here (see Unit 21). Marshall, you will recall, argued that 'Scottish interests and Scottish sympathies were very deeply involved in Empire' and the idea of an imperial partnership with England formed a key part of Scottish identity in this period (Marshall, 1995, p. 387). Empire provided opportunities for many Scots, both at home and abroad. Only a minority, of course, will have joined Britain's imperial elite, but this was true of England too (B).

What of Cannadine's final point (D)? Since this unit has concentrated on industry and empire, there has been little that is relevant to Cannadine's concern with empire as an 'imaginative construct'. One point, however, might be made. In terms of the course themes, the unit has focused on producers and consumers. It has examined Dundee's consumption of raw jute and production of jute sacking, and the organisation of this process. It has also explored how the city was shaped and defined by the process of production. The theme of beliefs and ideologies has, however, also intruded in places, for instance when discussing tariffs versus free trade or the employment of women in the mills and factories. When contemporaries discussed such issues, the debate was framed by beliefs about how trade should be organised or the proper role of women. One such set of beliefs concerned empire. As we saw in the debate about tariffs, to justify their arguments participants drew on imagery that defined the proper relationship between colonies and metropole. I picked out the way their language used parent–child images; on other occasions, discussions might be framed in terms of 'master and servant'. Part of the fury of some of the participants in the debate surely came from a feeling that Calcutta was not fulfilling its function of serving Dundee. Their 'imaginative construct' of the empire placed Dundee at the centre and Calcutta on the periphery, even though, by 1900, Dundee was very much the smaller of the two.

REFERENCES

Arnold, A.J. (1995) 'Should historians trust late nineteenth century company financial statements?', *Business History*, vol. 38, pp. 40–54.

Bayly, C.A. (1989) *Imperial Meridian. The British Empire and the World, 1780–1830*, London, Longman.

Cain, P.J. and Hopkins, A.G. (1993a) *British Imperialism. Innovation and Expansion, 1688–1914*, London, Longman.

Cain, P.J. and Hopkins, A.G. (1993b) *British Imperialism. Crisis and Deconstruction, 1914–1990*, London, Longman.

Dundee Photographic Survey (1915) vol. 1 *Industry*, Dundee.

Dundee Social Union (1905) *Report on the Housing and Social Conditions in Dundee*, Dundee. John Leng & Co.

Edelstein, M. (2004) 'Foreign investment, accumulation and empire, 1860–1914' in Floud, R. and Johnson, P. (eds) *The Cambridge Economic History of Modern Britain*, vol. 2, *Economic Maturity, 1860–1939*, Cambridge, Cambridge University Press.

Gauldie, E. (1987) 'The Dundee jute industry' in Butt, J. and Ponting, K. (eds) *Scottish Textile History*, Aberdeen, Aberdeen University Press.

Gordon, E. (1991) *Women and the Labour Movement in Scotland, 1850–1914*, Oxford, Clarendon Press.

Halley, J.R.L. (1980) *A History of Halley's Mill, 1822–1980*, Dundee, Wm Halley & Sons.

Hobsbawm, E.J. (1968) *Industry and Empire*, London, Penguin.

Lazonick, W. (1991) *Business Organization and the Myth of the Market Economy*, Cambridge, Cambridge University Press.

Lenman, B. and Donaldson, K. (1971) 'Partners' incomes, investment and diversification in the Scottish linen area, 1850–1921', *Business History*, vol. 13, pp. 1–18.

Marshall, P.J. (1995) 'Imperial Britain', *Journal of Imperial and Commonwealth History*, vol. 23, pp. 379–94.

Miskell, L. and Whatley, C.A. (1999) '"Juteopolis" in the making: linen and the industrial transformation of Dundee, *c.*1820–1850', *Textile History*, vol. 30, pp. 176–98.

Porter, A. (1990) 'The South African War (1899–1902): context and motive reconsidered', *Journal of African History*, vol. 31, no. 1, pp. 43–57.

Rodger, R. (1985) 'Employment, wages and poverty in the Scottish cities, 1841–1914' in Gordon, G. (ed.) *Perspectives on the Scottish City*, Aberdeen, Aberdeen University Press.

Sethia, T. (1996) 'The rise of the jute manufacturing industry in colonial India: a global perspective', *Journal of World History*, vol. 7, pp. 71–99.

Stewart, G.T. (1998) *Jute and Empire. The Calcutta Jute Wallahs and the Landscapes of Empire*, Manchester, Manchester University Press.

'The Photographic Survey' (1905) *Dundee Yearbook*, Dundee, John Leng & Co.

Wainwright, E.M. (2005) 'Dundee's jute mills and factories: spaces of production, surveillance and discipline', *Scottish Geographical Journal*, vol. 121, no. 2, pp. 121–40.

Robin Mackie and Annika Mombauer

INTRODUCTION

This unit will look at European imperialism in Africa at the end of the nineteenth century. In this, as in the previous two units, we start from Europe: it is a study of why Europeans conquered Africa and how they ruled it. An African history of European imperialism would be very different. The unit explores some of the background and reasons for the European conquest of Africa, and, using the experience of the Congo as an example, the consequences of these motivations for how colonies were ruled and exploited. It finishes by exploring the campaign in Europe against the worst excesses in the Congo. All three course themes are relevant: state formation is important when we examine some of the motivations for expansion; producers and consumers is significant when we turn to the hopes that Europeans placed in colonies and the 'opening' of Africa, and the reality of exploitation in the Congo; finally, beliefs and ideologies figures when we consider the underlying beliefs that formed the background to the conquest of Africa, and also the ideas of those who challenged European rule in the Congo. The unit is divided into five sections. The first will examine international rivalry in Africa in the 1880s, focusing on the Berlin Africa Conference of 1884/85; while the second explores Germany's colonial policy under Bismarck. The final three sections will consider, in turn, how the Congo Free State was created as an independent state controlled by Leopold II of Belgium, how the colony was governed and exploited, and the campaign against atrocities in the Congo that finally led to its takeover by Belgium.

THE 'SCRAMBLE FOR AFRICA' AND THE BERLIN AFRICA CONFERENCE OF 1884/85

So far this block has focused on British imperialism. You will recall from Unit 21 that one reason for British expansion was rivalry with other European powers, particularly in Africa. In Unit 21, we noted how rapidly the continent was divided up in the 1880s and 1890s and that Britain took the largest share in what has been described as 'the scramble for Africa'. If you look at the map in Plate 23.1 in the *Visual Sources*, you will also note colonies belonging to France, Portugal and Spain. They too, like Britain, were old imperial powers – all four countries already ruled colonies in the period discussed in Block 4. However, the map also shows colonies belonging to Germany and Italy, and a curiously named state in the middle of Africa: the 'Congo State'. This last was effectively the private empire of Leopold II, king of the Belgians – but it was not a Belgian colony. Germany, Italy and Belgium had never possessed overseas empires.

EXERCISE

Identify the colonies acquired by Germany and the territory of the Congo Free State in Plate 23.1 in the *Visual Sources*. Using the chronology in the *Course Guide*, note the dates that the German colonies in Africa were established and when the Free State was proclaimed.

Spend about 5–10 minutes on this exercise.

SPECIMEN ANSWER

There are four German colonies: South-West Africa (now Namibia), Togo, Kamerun (now Cameroon) and German East Africa (now Tanzania, although in each case the frontiers are slightly different). All of them were declared German 'protectorates' in 1884 and 1885. The Congo Free State was also established in 1885.

DISCUSSION

Don't worry; you are not required to learn all these dates by heart! This exercise is merely intended to acquaint you with some of the territories that you will be learning about in this unit and the next, and with the way Europeans divided the African continent among themselves. In particular, you may have been surprised by just how rapidly colonies were claimed in the 1884/85 period (of course, as we shall see, it took much longer to establish control – drawing lines on a map was one thing; governing was another).

The Berlin Africa Conference

The interest of new imperial powers in Africa inevitably created tensions between the European states. To a certain extent, German activity was a response to British and French expansion; in turn, it stimulated it. As you know from Unit 21, contemporaries and historians have argued about the causes of expansion in this period, and whether they should be sought in long-term trends, such as changes in the world economy, or specific events, such as the crises in Egypt or South Africa. However, when we consider the reasons why new imperial powers acquired colonies, some factors are more likely to be important than others. Britain or France might have been responding to crises in Africa, but this is less likely of Germany or Italy, or of Leopold II of Belgium, since they had few interests there. Explanations for why they acquired colonies are more likely to be found in Europe.

Much of this unit will explore the reasons why Germany acquired colonies and why the Congo Free State was created, but let us first look a bit more at *how* the division of Africa happened. A key moment was the Berlin Africa Conference, which ran from 15 November 1884 to 26 February 1885. A direct result of the conference was the proclamation of the Congo Free State in July of that year.

The immediate background to the conference lay in events at the mouth of the Congo river, where agents working for France and for Leopold's Association Internationale du Congo (the AIC – you will learn more about this organisation later in the unit) were active. In an attempt to forestall other countries claiming the region, the British government proposed a treaty to Portugal (which had claimed rights in the Congo, including control of the mouth of the river, since the sixteenth century) recognising Portuguese sovereignty over the coast in exchange for guarantees relating to British trade. In turn, Leopold II, concerned that the AIC was being squeezed out and anxious to win allies, offered a deal to the French: if the AIC ever decided to abandon their trading stations, they would cede them to France. The French were only too happy to accept. Portugal was widely regarded as a British satellite, and Britain and France had been at loggerheads in a number of colonial crises. Only two years after the British occupation of Egypt in 1882, the scene seemed set for another confrontation.

It was in this situation that Bismarck, the chancellor of Germany, proposed an international conference (you will find more information on Bismarck in Unit 19). The idea of a conference originated with Portugal, but was taken up by Bismarck, who saw it as an opportunity to curb Britain's claims to an 'informal empire' over much of Africa. Bismarck wanted to have the conference in Berlin, ideally timed to coincide with German elections in October, although he also offered the French prime minister, Jules Ferry, the option of convening the conference in Paris. The latter was horrified at the thought of having the victors of the Battle of Sedan[2] in Paris, and Berlin was agreed upon as the venue (Robinson, 1988, p. 8). Bismarck's interests were much more focused on European power politics than on colonial aspirations. Holding the conference in Berlin was seen as investing it with an authority derived from Germany, the powerful country at the heart of Europe that was part of the Three Emperors' League and the Triple Alliance (Germany, Austria-Hungary and Italy). Bismarck hoped to intimidate the British into attending. Britain's presence at the conference would

> acknowledge before the German people the advent of German world power in the face of the greatest of maritime empires. The Chancellor's allies had to come to Berlin to show the English that Germany's preponderance in Europe counted overseas. Thus, Bismarck's Conference was planned as a ritual drama signifying a change in seniority between sibling nations.
>
> (Robinson, 1988, p. 8)

As such, it is possible to see the conference at least partly as an aspect of Bismarck's continual attempt to build a German national state.

Bismarck invited representatives of the great powers, France, Britain, Italy, Austria-Hungary, Russia and the USA, as well as those of smaller states, Belgium, Denmark, the Netherlands, Portugal, Spain, Sweden and Turkey. All accepted: the growing competition between the European states in Africa meant that none could afford not to attend. The conference is often described as 'partitioning Africa'. In fact, the avowed purpose of the conference was humanitarian: to suppress slavery and to 'open' Africa to trade. In this period, great hopes were placed in the latter: it was believed that free trade would

---

[2] Germany had defeated France in the Franco-Prussian War of 1870/71, and one of that war's battles took place at Sedan.

bring Africa the benefits of European 'civilisation'. The General Act of the Conference guaranteed freedom of navigation on the Congo and Niger rivers, agreed on measures to end the internal African slave trade and attempted to prevent the use of African soldiers in European wars (Hildebrand, 1989, pp. 15–16). Frontiers were agreed for a free-trade zone in the area of central Africa covering the Congo basin but stretching right across the continent to the Indian Ocean; if the AIC was recognised as a state within this area, it was mainly to prevent any European country claiming it. Finally, the delegates attempted to regulate how European powers acquired colonies: future claims should be based on 'effective occupation' and not simply on vague announcements of paramountcy.

However, illustrations such as that in Figure 23.1, which appeared during the conference in a German journal, certainly created the impression that the fate of Africa was being decided. Delegates are seen discussing under a giant map of Africa and it is noticeable (as you may have spotted from the list of invitees) that no Africans were present. The conference also did not stop the process of partition. In the months following the conference, further colonies were proclaimed and Leopold II moved to establish the Congo Free State. If anything, by focusing attention on Africa and establishing some ground rules, the conference hastened the 'scramble'. To contemporaries, it was clear that Africa was being carved up.

EXERCISE

The cartoon in Figure 23.2 appeared in *Punch* during the Berlin conference. Describe what it depicts, and analyse what it says about British attitudes to Germany's colonial expansion.

Spend about 5–10 minutes on this exercise.

SPECIMEN ANSWER

The cartoon depicts a globe in the form of a Christmas pudding, which two rather stout boys are eating. On the right, taller and slightly overpowering, is Bismarck (characterised by his moustache). On his plate is already a large piece of the pudding, but he is leaning across to take another piece, while the other diner, who has a more modest piece of pudding on his fork, looks on in astonishment. In the cartoon, Bismarck (representing Germany) is shown as greedily helping himself to too big a portion: more than his fair share, and perhaps even more than he can handle. In the eyes of the cartoonist, Britain clearly is threatened by this newcomer.

DISCUSSION

The piece of pudding that Bismarck already has is labelled Angra Pequena, which is a harbour in what became German South-West Africa, while that he is taking is labelled New Guinea. Although New Guinea is not in Africa, part of it was claimed by the German New Guinea Company in 1884 and the cartoon only makes sense against the background of the Berlin conference. British concerns may seem slightly hypocritical in view of the size of the British empire, but the anxieties expressed were real enough. But why did Bismarck feel the need to challenge the other colonial powers? In the next section, we will look at the motivation behind his colonial policy of the 1880s.

Figure 23.1 Congo Conference, Berlin, 15 November 1884 to 26 February 1885, wood engraving after a drawing by Adalbert von Rössler from *Über Land und Meer*, Vol. 53, 1883/85. Photo: AKG, London. The picture shows European and American diplomats discussing the future of Africa at the Berlin Conference in 1884/85. Bismarck is seated third from the right, facing the large map of Africa.

PUNCH, OR THE LONDON CHARIVARI.—January 10, 1885.

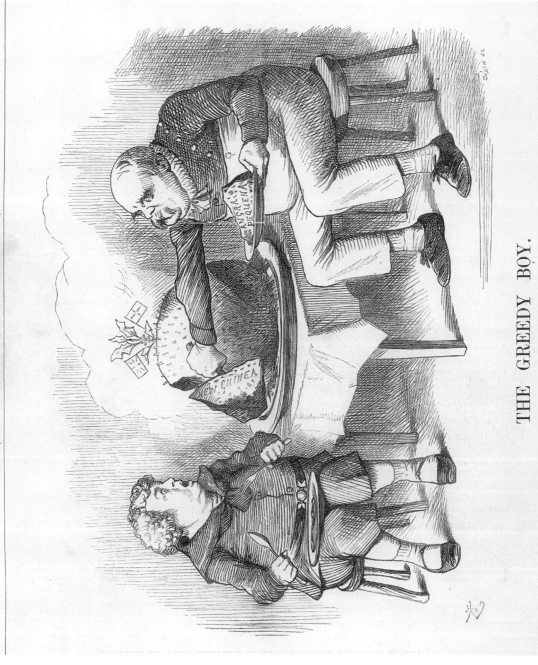

THE GREEDY BOY.

Figure 23.2 John Tenniel, 'The Greedy Boy', cartoon published in *Punch*, 10 January 1885, showing Britain and Germany (in the shape of Bismarck) carving up the globe. Photo: Mary Evans Picture Library. Note that the cartoon makes reference to one by Gillray, published in 1805 (see Figure 17.4)

GERMAN COLONIALISM UNDER BISMARCK: 'MY MAP OF AFRICA IS IN EUROPE'

The key to understanding the motivation of the German chancellor, Otto von Bismarck, is to place his colonial policy in a European context. Germany had only been unified into the *Deutsches Reich* (German empire) in 1871, following three wars (against Denmark, Austria and France) in which Germany had upset the European balance of power and had made many potential enemies. Bismarck, as chancellor of the new Reich, was haunted by what he called his 'nightmare of coalitions'. His worry was that Germany's neighbours, and in particular the disgruntled French, would form alliances against Germany and perhaps launch another war. He made it clear to the other great powers that Germany did not strive for further territorial gain (by declaring Germany to be 'satiated'), and his policy focused on trying to avoid conflict with all other powers. At the same time, he was keen to foster disagreements between the other powers as a way of ensuring that these would not conclude those dreaded alliances.

One way of keeping out of international disputes was not to get involved in colonial ventures. In 1881, Bismarck declared: 'As long as I am Imperial Chancellor we will not be undertaking any colonial policy' (quoted in Canis, 2002, p. 24). The sudden acquisition of colonies in 1884 was therefore a dramatic change of policy. Why did Bismarck, who had so far opposed any colonial expansion, suddenly have a change of heart and, for a brief period in the mid-1880s, embrace expansion?

Bismarck's imperialism

One answer to this conundrum was provided in 1970 by a leading German historian, Hans-Ulrich Wehler. In his book *Imperialismus* and in an article in an English-language journal, *Past & Present*, Wehler suggested that the reasons for Bismarck's imperialism could be found in the internal situation in Germany.

EXERCISE

Two short extracts from Wehler's article 'Bismarck's imperialism, 1862–1890', *Past & Present*, vol. 48, August 1970, pp. 119–55, are available on the course website. Read them now.

Spend about 10 minutes on this exercise.

Wehler argues that the new German empire was destabilised by rapid and erratic industrialisation within a hierarchical and authoritarian social and political system. In the first extract, Wehler explains why he thinks Bismarck resorted to imperialism in 1884: there was an economic downturn and he saw clear political advantages (there was an election in October 1884). The second extract is from the conclusion to the article. Here Wehler sums up his argument in terms of defending a conservative political system in a period of rapid economic and social change.

Wehler's theory is often described as 'social imperialism'. As you can imagine, it has proved to be highly controversial, not least for the suggestions about continuities in German history that Wehler explicitly makes (you may have noted the reference to anti-Semitism in the first paragraph).

EXERCISE

The debate continues today. Read the section from Katharine Anne Lerman's *Bismarck. Profiles in Power*, Longman, London, 2004, pp. 214–17, in the secondary sources on the course website. The extract considers Bismarck's colonial policy in the years 1883–85. Lerman argues that Bismarck's motives for pursuing a colonial policy at that time 'have probably exercised historians more than contemporaries or, indeed, Bismarck himself'. What possible reasons for Bismarck's sudden adoption of colonial policy does she mention? Underline the different arguments and summarise them. For each point, consider how convincing Lerman finds them.

Spend about 30–45 minutes on this exercise.

SPECIMEN ANSWER

There are four different possible arguments:

- Bismarck may have been responding to domestic pressure and to a growing popular movement in favour of colonial acquisitions. However, Lerman considers it unlikely that Bismarck was driven by domestic interest groups.

- He may have used colonial policy as a way of distracting public attention away from domestic problems (colonialism as 'a kind of "social imperialist" device'). Lerman is not persuaded that Bismarck saw colonial acquisitions as a 'panacea' for domestic problems.

- Bismarck may have been motivated by international considerations, perhaps as a way of bringing about a rapprochement with France. Bismarck's collaboration with the French prime minister, Jules Ferry, during the Berlin Africa Conference might point in this direction. Lerman does not say if this is a convincing argument or not, but points out that the domestic situation in France worked against such a rapprochement becoming reality.

- His colonial policy may also have been driven by his desire to please the German crown prince, who favoured a colonial policy. This interpretation also links Bismarck's colonial policy with his hostile attitude to Britain. Again, Lerman does not dismiss or endorse this argument.

DISCUSSION

In this extract, Lerman is advancing a wide range of reasons for Bismarck's imperialism, only the first two of which overlap with Wehler's arguments. She is clearly not persuaded by the social imperialist case and suggests instead a number of short-term foreign policy factors. To some extent, of course, discussion of Bismarck's motives must involve a measure of speculation. It is also likely that it was the result of a combination of the factors, rather than just one single reason. However, the elections of 1884 almost certainly had some part in his decision. His statement that 'the whole colonial thing is a fraud, but we need it for the elections' (quoted in Fröhlich, 1994, p. 33), suggests, moreover, that he may not really have abandoned his previously hostile stance towards colonial expansion.

EXERCISE

In the same extract, Lerman suggests that Bismarck abandoned imperialism almost as quickly as he had embraced it. What reasons does she give for his loss of interest? Why did colonies prove a contentious issue for Bismarck?

Spend about 5–10 minutes on this exercise.

SPECIMEN ANSWER

- 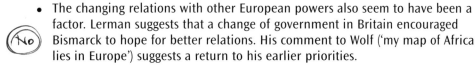 Expense seems to have been the main reason for this change of heart. Bismarck had underestimated the cost to Germany of administering colonies, not least the need to increase taxes at home. Colonies gave the *Reichstag* (parliament) more budgetary powers (this is because the *Reichstag* had to vote for all budget matters and could also veto expenses, as it did in the case of colonies), and this was a potential problem for Bismarck, who did not want to see the *Reichstag's* powers extended.

- The changing relations with other European powers also seem to have been a factor. Lerman suggests that a change of government in Britain encouraged Bismarck to hope for better relations. His comment to Wolf ('my map of Africa lies in Europe') suggests a return to his earlier priorities.

DISCUSSION

Lerman's explanation for Bismarck's imperialism is very different from Wehler's. Whereas Wehler concentrates on social and economic reasons, Lerman gives precedence to political and diplomatic ones; whereas Wehler highlights long-term, underlying factors, Lerman emphasises short-term, contingent ones. As you will recall from Unit 21, theories operating at different levels may not be contradictory: 'grand theories' may provide us with useful insights while not explaining particular events as well as more focused explanations. Nevertheless, Lerman's point about Bismarck not being too 'exercised' by colonies may be the significant one: the whole episode was a very short one in a career in which European power politics was the overriding concern.

However, if Bismarck rapidly lost interest, this was not true of the various colonial pressure groups. While, to Bismarck, colonialism had been, as he once put it, 'a hoax', it was 'a hoax that he admittedly needed for election purposes. Worse, he found that the genie of imperialism which he had released could not be put back into the bottle' (Berghahn, 1994, p. 269). From the early 1880s on, public pressure groups were set up to lobby for colonial expansion. The Kolonialverein (Colonial Society) was founded in 1882. With its many publications, it aimed to popularise the quest for colonies and put substantial pressure on the German government to build up an overseas empire. Other pressure groups soon joined it, including the Pan-German League. Pressure also came from economic circles such as firms trading with West Africa, chambers of commerce, and financiers, as well as from economists, intellectuals and university professors (Kennedy, 1980, pp. 168–9). Heinrich von Treitschke, the German historian, famously declared: 'We want and ought to claim our share in the domination of the earth by the white race' (quoted in Kennedy, 1980, p. 169). Many of these people joined the Kolonialverein, and its popularity was such that it had attracted 100,000 members by 1885.

However, there was also opposition to Germany's colonial expansion, particularly among the Social Democrats and the Catholic Centre Party. In

Reichstag debates and critical publications, these parties made their opposition known, particularly, as we will see in Unit 24, in relation to the way native peoples were treated by German settlers in the colonies.

Summary

The unit has so far looked at a key event in the process by which Africa was divided by European imperial powers, the Berlin Africa Conference, and at the background to Germany's sudden colonial expansion. We will return in the next unit to German imperialism. But first we turn to the most direct outcome of the Berlin Africa Conference: the Congo Free State.

LEOPOLD II, BELGIUM AND THE CONGO

If Bismarck is the central figure in the history of the German colonies, Leopold II, King of the Belgians, plays a similar role in the history of the Congo. But there the parallel ends. Bismarck was chancellor and, effectively, in charge of German domestic and foreign policy. Leopold was a constitutional monarch with, on paper, very limited powers. Bismarck, as we have seen, was usually a reluctant imperialist; Leopold had no such doubts. On the other hand, there were many groups in Germany that wanted Germany to acquire colonies; by contrast, most Belgians were – at least at first – extremely sceptical about their king's colonial adventure. Nevertheless, Leopold was rather more successful than Bismarck in getting the empire he wanted.

In the story of how Leopold II acquired an African empire, the key event was the Berlin Africa Conference. But before discussing how he used the conference (which he did not attend) to carve out what was, in effect, a private empire in the middle of Africa, let us first look at why Leopold II was so keen to acquire a colony and why most Belgians were not.

Different views of colonies: Leopold II and Belgium

The Belgium of which Leopold became king in 1865 was a relatively new creation. As you will know from Blocks 1 and 2, the territory which is now Belgium had been part of the Burgundian lands and then part of the Spanish and later Austrian Netherlands. During the French Revolution and under Napoleon it had been part of France, and at the Treaty of Vienna following Waterloo it had been given to the Netherlands to create a strong buffer state to the north of France. However, in 1830–31, as part of the wave of nation building discussed in Unit 19, the people had risen up against Dutch rule and had established an independent state. Belgium was born.

The creation of a new state in the middle of western Europe was, of course, a matter of great interest to its neighbours. Britain, France and Prussia were all sceptical about the future of the new state and anxious to prevent it falling under the influence of their rivals. Part of the process of reassuring the great powers was finding an acceptable king. After a first candidate was rejected as too close to France, Leopold II's father, Leopold of Saxe-Coburg, was proposed and accepted in 1831 (Emerson, 1979, pp. 1–3). In 1839, the Dutch finally recognised the new state and all the major European powers guaranteed to respect Belgium as 'an independent and perpetually neutral state' (it was the breach of this guarantee by Germany in 1914 that provided the cause for Britain's entry into the First World War).

Both Belgium and its monarchy therefore existed as a balancing act. Belgium needed to reassure the powers that it would indeed remain neutral and independent. Leopold was selected as a compromise candidate: a German prince and an uncle to Queen Victoria, in 1832 he went on to marry a French princess. Unlike other monarchs, he did not inherit the throne, but had been installed by the new state's constituent assembly, the National Congress. The constitution set clear limits to his power. In his eyes, both the new state and his throne were always vulnerable.

These preoccupations were inherited by his son, who succeeded to the throne in 1865. For Leopold II, however, they became closely linked to the search for colonies. His father had also seen the acquisition of colonies as one way of strengthening the state, but his prudence made him cautious. For Leopold II, they became something of an obsession. Before becoming king, he travelled widely, including trips to the eastern Mediterranean, French North Africa, Egypt, India, Singapore, the Dutch East Indies and China. His observation of overseas countries and imperial rule was backed up by extensive research and reading. Even before becoming king, his speeches and writings reflected this interest. His first speech to the Belgian senate in 1855, aged just twenty, concerned Belgian trade in the Ottoman empire.

> **Leopold II** (1835–1909) became the second king of Belgium in 1865. As a constitutional monarch, his powers within Belgium were limited, although he had considerable influence on foreign and defence issues. From 1885, until it was handed over to Belgium in 1908, he was also absolute ruler of the Congo Free State.

EXERCISE

Why was Leopold II so anxious to acquire colonies? Read the four extracts in Anthology Document 6.12, 'Speeches and documents of Leopold II, king of the Belgians, and answer the following questions. What benefits did Leopold see in imperial expansion? What differences and similarities are there between the texts? As usual when reading a primary source, think about the nature of the source and its context.

There are a number of ways of organising your answers to questions such as these, and you may well have done this differently from the specimen answer.

Spend about 1 hour on this exercise.

SPECIMEN ANSWER

All four are taken from a book by one of Leopold II's ardent supporters: hardly an unbiased source. However, they are all direct quotes from Leopold II or his papers and as such can be taken as his words. Although the information on the context of each extract is limited, it is clear that at least three are from very public speeches or documents and that even the letter from which (c) is taken is not really a personal letter. All certainly read like public pronouncements. The four statements were, however, made to different audiences and at widely dispersed times, which may explain the differences between them.

With regard to the benefits that Leopold expected, it is notable that sometimes the benefits were presented in terms of Belgium and sometimes in terms of the colony. In the first extract, the advantages listed are all for Belgium. The gains expected are economic (trade, emigration, lower taxes) and political ('a certain increase in power …'). In the second, by contrast, it is Africa that is expected to gain from the European 'opening' of Africa, although the benefits ('civilisation') may seem rather vague. Belgium is 'happy and satisfied with its lot' – all that Leopold is seeking is 'honour'.

The third extract again focuses on Belgium. In some respects, the sentiments expressed contrast strongly with extract (b), particularly in the apocalyptic assessment of the risks Belgium runs if it does not expand overseas. Again, what Belgium stands to gain is primarily economic, although social tensions are predicted if it does not avail itself of this opportunity. The final extract is the first to explicitly list benefits to both the Congo and Belgium, and includes economic and more intangible benefits: 'moral' improvement for the people of the Congo and greater 'luster' and prestige for Belgium.

DISCUSSION

The benefits of empire may have been presented differently in each extract (though the economic gain to Belgium is a recurring theme), however, there is a great deal of continuity in how Leopold II chose to present his role. In the first extract he talks of 'family duty', in the second he states that he has 'no other ambition than to serve [Belgium] well'. Similar phrases also appear in the latter two extracts. The theme of service to his country was one which figured in many of Leopold's public statements. In part, this may no doubt be dismissed as the sort of platitude expected of a constitutional monarch. Yet (as you will see when you view section 2 of DVD 3) the close identification of nation and dynasty was a feature of Leopold's thinking. It is also apparent that Leopold was quite willing not only to serve his country but also to guide it.

Many of the views expressed by Leopold about colonies were commonplace in this period and it would not be too difficult to find similar statements by public figures in Britain, France or Germany. Yet it would be wrong to think that everyone believed that overseas expansion would benefit the colonial power and, indeed, in late nineteenth-century Belgium, many were sceptical about Leopold's plans. This was partly due to the same insecurity that made their king so keen on expansion: Belgian statesmen feared antagonising their powerful neighbours and were only too aware how disputes over colonies were ratcheting up tensions between European states. Furthermore, many Belgians were far less convinced than Leopold of the economic advantages of colonial rule. Strong believers in free trade, they saw trade as the source of profits and overseas territories simply as a drain on resources. As one of the first countries to industrialise, Belgium prospered in the second half of the nineteenth century in spite of not possessing colonies. Why go to the trouble of acquiring them when Belgian goods sold so successfully in foreign markets? Finally, divisions within Belgium kept politics firmly fixed on internal issues. At first the National Assembly was dominated by the Liberal representatives of the urban upper-middle class. Over time, a conservative Catholic opposition developed, drawing support from rural areas and from the lower-middle class; by the 1870s and 1880s, they were challenging the Liberal hegemony. The major conflicts were about the role of the church, particularly in education. Later still, radical Liberals and Socialists challenged the other parties on economic and social issues. In all this, colonies seemed a mere distraction, particularly since they were closely associated in public opinion with a strong state and army, which, for a range of reasons, all distrusted (Lambert, 1999).

The Berlin Africa Conference and the creation of the Congo Free State

As a constitutional monarch, Leopold could not dictate state policy. In the first decade of his reign, his proposals for empire building were courteously received by the country's leaders, but largely ignored. It was developments in Africa that created an opportunity.

As you know from Unit 21, European interest in Central Africa was awakened in the 1860s and 1870s by the travels of explorers such as David Livingstone and Henry Morton Stanley. One shock was the extent of what was termed the 'Arab' slave trade in eastern and central Africa (most of the traders were in fact from the east African coast, although some of the slaves they captured did end up in the Arab world). Ending the trade became, along with opening the interior to commerce and spreading Christianity, one of the goals of a humanitarian strand in empire building. In the 1870s, Leopold courted the leading figures in this movement. In 1876, he organised a Geographical Conference in Brussels to which were invited leading explorers from across Europe (you have read part of the speech Leopold made to this conference in Anthology Document 6.12b). When this conference established an International Africa Association, it was natural that its headquarters should be established in Belgium and Leopold elected its first chairman.

On Stanley's return after crossing Africa, Leopold lost no time in establishing contact with him. Stanley was convinced of the enormous economic value of the territories he had crossed, but in London, although he was received as a hero, the government showed little interest in acquiring a new African colony. In the late 1870s, the British still hoped to maintain informal control over much of Africa without shouldering the expense of direct rule. Leopold, on the other hand, was enthusiastic and agreed to fund a further expedition to explore the economic potential of the region. Stanley was instructed to establish trading posts and sign treaties with local chiefs. This was not done in the name of Belgium, however, but in that of the successor organisation to the IAA, the

Association Internationale du Congo, the AIC, which you encountered earlier in this unit. In the early 1880s, therefore, as European states competed for pieces of Africa, a non-state organisation, the AIC, with its distinctive yellow star flag, was establishing itself on the lower Congo.

It was to this organisation that the Berlin conference gave responsibility for opening the Congo basin, stamping out the slave trade and ensuring free trade. Leopold II's success at the conference was partly due to some nimble diplomacy, but perhaps also to the lack of knowledge and interest in Africa displayed by the other participants. As you know, the conference took place against the background of complicated international tensions, and for many countries the main goal was to check the ambitions of their rivals; Leopold's AIC seemed like a harmless, altruistic (and perhaps also short-term) alternative. Delegates showed little interest in the structure of the organisation, which was, in fact, entirely under Leopold's control. In May 1885, now established on the ground at the mouth of the Congo, the AIC changed its name again to the État Indépendant du Congo (Congo Free State).

Summary

In this section, we have looked at why Leopold was so keen to acquire a colony and at how the Berlin Africa Conference in 1884/85 gave him the opportunity to do so without the official backing of his country, Belgium. You will have noted that as well as arguments for empire, there were also some against it (some of which echoed the views of British free traders and of Hobson that you encountered in Unit 21). Before returning to the critics of imperialism, the unit will next examine how the Congo Free State was ruled and exploited.

THE CONGO FREE STATE

Establishing control

The Congo basin that Leopold II acquired at the Berlin conference had only recently been explored by Europeans. It was only with Stanley's 1874–77 expedition across Africa that the course of the Congo river was properly understood (see Figure 23.3). During the 1880s and 1890s, the new state sent a number of expeditions into the interior of Africa to push out the boundaries of the territory it claimed. As part of the process of asserting control, 'stations' were established – often little more than collections of huts beside the river controlled by small groups of African soldiers under the command of a European officer.

From the beginning, control of the river was seen as the key to the interior of Africa. The Congo river and its tributaries form a vast river network that extends through much of the territory claimed by the new state, a network which had long been used by African traders. In the east, caravan routes linked

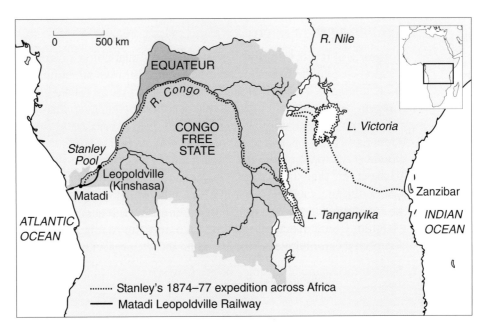

Figure 23.3   Map of central Africa showing Stanley's expedition across Africa and the boundaries of the Congo Free State

it to the Great Lakes and the Indian Ocean. In the west, too, access to this river network from the coast was overland, since a series of rapids stretching 250 miles blocked the lower Congo. One of the first tasks the new state set itself, therefore, was to build a railway round the rapids to the Stanley Pool (now the Malebo Pool) above the rapids. Work was started on the railway in 1890 and was completed in 1898. Only with the completion of the railway did it really become possible to establish control in the interior. So weak, indeed, was the Free State in parts of the upper Congo that, for a period in the 1880s, the most powerful of the east coast slave traders, known to Europeans as Tippu Tip, was appointed a provincial governor as a means of establishing authority. As elsewhere in Africa, the imposition of European control met with resistance from African inhabitants, and this was augmented by major rebellions among the African troops of the new state, the *force publique*, so that fighting continued in some part of the state's territory for almost the entire time until it was taken over by Belgium in 1908.

The administration of this huge territory was rudimentary. Local officials were given almost complete authority over their districts and ruled through a combination of brute force and deals with local chiefs. Some military officers were seconded from the Belgian army; others were recruited all over Europe. As well as the servants of the state, there were a few traders and missionaries, but, even in 1908, there were still only around 3,000 Europeans in the colony, of whom about 1,700 were Belgian (Stengers and Vansina, 1985, p. 351). Major decisions were made in Brussels, by an administration that was completely separate from the Belgian state and answered only to the king.

Exploiting the Congo

As you will recall, Leopold II was convinced that colonies would be profitable. In fact, despite the new state's limited administrative structure, in the first years it operated at a loss. When the Free State was first established in 1885, the Belgian parliament had insisted that accounts be kept separate, and Leopold had assured parliament that he would not need subsidies. At first, the king drew on his large personal fortune and private loans. By the late 1880s, however, the pressure on the royal finances was such that the queen was heard to exclaim: 'Mais Léopold, tu vas nous ruiner avec ton Congo!' (But Leopold, you will ruin us with your Congo!) (Ascherson, 1999 [1963], p. 148). In 1890, he was forced to ask the Belgian state for a loan. It seemed inevitable that Belgium would eventually have to take over the running of the colony and that Leopold's colonial plans would saddle the country with an expensive liability.

In fact, the financial fortunes of the new state were transformed in the mid-1890s. To understand how this happened, we need to look at the colony's exports (see Table 23.1).

Table 23.1   **Exports from the Congo in tons and as a percentage of total exports, 1887–1913**

	Exports of gathered products, 1887–1913 (in 1,000 tons)					Percentage of total exports from Congo (by value)	
	Palm oil	**Palm kernels**	**Ivory**	**Rubber**	**Copal**	**Ivory**	**Rubber**
1887	1.0	2.9	–	–	–	41	6
1890	2.3	6.5	0.2	0.1	–	56	6
1892	0.9	3.0	0.2	0.1	–	67	11
1895	1.8	4.9	0.3	0.6	–	53	26
1898	1.4	4.7	0.2	2.1	–	19	71
1900	1.6	4.8	0.2	5.3	–	11	84
1902	1.7	5.2	0.2	5.3	0.2	8	84
1904	1.7	4.5	0.1	4.8	0.9	10	84
1906	1.9	4.9	0.1	4.8	0.8	11	83
1908	2.1	5.2	0.2	4.5	1.6	12	75
1910	2.1	6.1	0.2	3.4	0.9	9	76
1911	2.2	6.7	0.2	3.4	2.1	10	62
1912	2.0	5.8	0.2	3.5	3.7	9	59
1913	1.8	6.6	0.2	3.5	4.1	not available	not available

(Sources: Peemans, 1975, p. 171; Nelson, 1994, pp. 56, 95; Vangroenweghe, 1986, Appendix)

EXERCISE

What does Table 23.1 tell us about quantities of exports? And what it does tell us about their relative value?

Spend about 20 minutes on this exercise.

[Consequences]

SPECIMEN ANSWER

The first thing of note is what relatively small amounts were involved (compare the figures above with Dundee's jute imports in Plate 22.1, for example). Yet the Congo was considered one of more valuable African colonies: such figures show how insignificant trade with most of Africa was in this period.

Use as part of "economic factors"

In terms of weight, palm products accounted for well over half the exports in most years. The percentage figures are in striking contrast. First ivory, then rubber, accounted for an enormous percentage of the value of exports. In 1892, the 200 tons of ivory exported accounted for 67 per cent of the total value of the Congo's exports. Six years later, a roughly similar tonnage was worth only 19 per cent of exports. The reason was the increasing importance of rubber, exports of which increased from 100 to 5,300 tons, and from 11 per cent of total exports to 84 per cent. Not until 1912 did the value of these two products fall below 70 per cent of total exports, by which point a new forest product, copal (a resin used in varnishes), was beginning to take their place.

Even though Europeans only penetrated central Africa in the 1870s, the Congo basin had long been tied into long-distance trade networks. You will recall from Unit 13 that west central Africa was the most important source of slaves for the New World and its relative importance grew as the trade moved southwards following abolition by Britain and other north European states. This was the first of a series of 'products' from the Congo that were of sufficiently high value to Europeans to justify high transport costs.

As the Atlantic slave trade finally began to decline in the second half of the nineteenth century, slaves were replaced by a new product – ivory: 'The material culture of Victorian society created an unprecedented new demand. Ivory became a staple of fashion and status, and was used for the crafting of piano keys, billiard balls, jewelry, snuffboxes, and little trinkets that embellished the parlors and dressing-tables of the wealthy' (Nelson, 1994, p. 48). The huge elephant herds of the savannah and the quality of African ivory made central Africa the source of a valuable commodity. While ivory could be obtained from African hunters relatively cheaply in the interior, prices on the coast rose dramatically. Labour, however, was needed to transport the ivory to the coast. Two major export routes were used: down the Congo river to the Stanley Pool and east from the Great Lakes to Indian Ocean ports such as Zanzibar. At first, both routes were controlled by Africans, who used slave labour to transport the ivory where river transport was not possible. The 'Arab' slave trade was based around supplying the demand for ivory in Europe. In their fight with the slavers, and in their efforts to win a greater share of the ivory trade, Europeans also needed labour to provide food and transport for their expeditions, and they too resorted to forced labour. At times, deals were struck with some of the slavers; elsewhere, liberated slaves (who were a long way from their peoples) were enrolled as soldiers or as porters. Death rates among both groups were very high.

By the 1890s, however, the ivory boom had passed. This was partly the result of rising costs. Elephant herds had been devastated and traders had to pay more for tusks. As one agent complained in 1892: 'The natives who gather it now know its value and it is more expensive ... there is hardly any ivory coming from areas where it can be purchased for a string of beads' (quoted in Nelson, 1994, p. 82). Once again, however, a central African product was found where there was such demand in Europe and America that high transport costs were not a barrier. Bicycle and later car tyres needed rubber, which grew wild in many tropical regions of Africa and South America. Until cultivated rubber reached markets in the late 1900s, there was enormous demand for wild rubber, and prices doubled between 1893 and 1904 (Vangroenweghe, 1986, Appendix). Like ivory, the rubber trade needed labour. Transport was less of an issue once the railway round the falls on the lower Congo linked the river network with the sea. But the rubber plants in the jungle needed to be tapped and the rubber brought to the stations for sale, and both tasks were labour-intensive.

In principle, rubber could have been obtained through trade. Emily Osborn shows that local networks of African producers and traders successfully competed with European merchants in supplying rubber in Upper Guinée in West Africa (Osborn, 2004). But paying for the rubber obviously reduced profits and in the Congo Free State (as in the neighbouring French Congo), officials resorted to forced labour. By declaring that in most of the Congo all 'vacant' land (that is land beyond the cultivated areas round villages) belonged to the state, the state claimed for itself wild products, including rubber. The local inhabitants were also required to pay a tax, which was to be paid in kind – both in food and in rubber. Furthermore, in large parts of the Congo basin, the state delegated the right to collect taxes to concessionary companies, which paid a levy for the privilege.

The results of this system have been documented for a number of regions, including the ABIR concession in Equateur province, in the heart of the tropical forests. ABIR stood for the Anglo-Belgian India Rubber and Exploration Company. It was founded in 1892 by a group of British and Belgian shareholders led by Colonel John Thomas North, whom Leopold II had met at a horserace in Ostend and persuaded to invest £40,000 in the venture (Harms, 1983, p. 128). The company was granted a huge concession and supplied with guns, ammunition and soldiers. In exchange, the Congo Free State was to get 50 per cent of the company's profits. In 1898, the company was reorganised, with the Free State taking over many of the shares. The profits were enormous: in 1900, the peak year, BF5,869,025 (£234,750) profit was made and the value of the shares had risen to fifty times their 1892 value (Vangroenweghe, 1986, p. 96).

To exploit its concession, ABIR established a number of posts, each with one or two European agents who commanded African soldiers and labourers. The agents were responsible for collecting rubber in their area. Although they were paid a salary, it was the commission on rubber collected that was lucrative; those who failed to meet their quotas were fined and were likely to be relieved of their posts (Harms, 1983, pp. 131–2). Every adult male was required to deliver a set amount of rubber as a tax. A small payment was made for the rubber, but the main incentive was fear. Under constant pressure from head office to increase the supply of rubber, local officials used imprisonment, brutal beatings and hostage taking to enforce compliance. When resistance resulted, punitive expeditions were sent to destroy villages (Vangroenweghe, 1986, ch. 6). As Robert Harms writes, 'Abir was a plundering and tribute-collecting empire of the crudest sort' (Harms, 1983, p. 125), not dissimilar in its operations from the marauding slaving expeditions the Congo Free State had been set up to destroy.

The short-term profits to be made from operating in such a way were enormous. According to one calculation, in 1897 ABIR could deliver rubber to the Antwerp market for BF1.35 a kilo, where it would sell for between BF8 and 10 (Harms, 1983, p. 130). But profits depended on regular supplies and high prices, and both came under threat after 1900. This was partly due to a fall in prices as cheap, good-quality rubber from plantations in south-east Asia entered the market. Even before that, however, the rubber collection system in the ABIR concession was breaking down. The problem was that the rush to collect rubber destroyed stocks: the desperate African labourers often damaged the plants and the European officers had no incentive to preserve them or plant new ones, since they only stayed a year or two in Africa. By 1904, large areas of the concession were not producing any rubber. Attempting to maintain production, the company's officers resorted to ever more brutal methods, but to no avail: production in 1905 was less than half that in 1903 (Harms, 1975, p. 86). By 1906, the company was keen to abandon the concession.

| EXERCISE | Samuel Nelson concludes his book *Colonialism in the Congo Basin* by arguing that the dominant feature of colonial enterprise in the Congo was the search for quick profits, and that this search 'hinged upon three main conditioning factors: the world market, the natural environment and its resources, and the participation of large numbers of African workers in the colonial economy' (Nelson, 1994, p. 196). |

1   How helpful is this analysis in understanding the economic history of the Congo Free State?

2   What does this analysis suggest about the longer-term stability of the Free State economy?

Spend about 10–15 minutes on this exercise.

| SPECIMEN ANSWER | 1   Nelson's three factors can clearly be identified in the ivory and rubber booms. It was demand for ivory and later rubber that caused the high prices which made the gathering of these products profitable. The word 'gathered' is significant (the same term was used in Table 23.1): ivory and rubber were not cultivated or manufactured. Their existence might be regarded as an accident of nature. Finally, labour to gather and transport the products was crucial. One reason that such commodities were so cheap was that this labour was paid very little. This |

was not the only reason profits were made: the price difference between Europe and Africa was such that it was viable even where market wages were paid. But labour was particularly cheap in the Congo because it was forced.

2   Looking at the economy in these terms highlights the causes of instability. It was the combination of the three conditioning factors that made ivory and rubber so profitable. When prices fell and supplies dried up, exports collapsed.

DISCUSSION

One might compare the Free State regime with the plantation economies discussed in Block 4. Then, too, an economic system was built on the ruthless exploitation of natural and human resources. However, demand for sugar and cotton was sustained and the products were cultivated. Plantation owners had incentives to plan for the long term and this affected their behaviour. Similar incentives were not at work in the early years of European colonisation in the Congo and producers made little effort to conserve or replace natural resources. One might talk of a plunder economy.

The use of forced labour was not unique to the Congo. British and French colonies also used tax systems to force Africans to work for low wages. Contemporary writers identified a 'labour problem' in Africa, which they defined in racist terms – Africans were 'lazy' and needed to be forced to work. Brutality was commonplace. Yet, partly because many African colonies did not possess products that Europeans wanted, and partly because there were fewer controls on the Free State than on other colonial regimes, it seems that the Congo was worse than elsewhere.

EXERCISE

Anthology Document 6.14, 'Roger Casement's *Congo Report*, 11 December 1903', is an extract from a report on a journey made in 1904 by Roger Casement, the British consul, to the Equateur province, where ABIR had its concession. Read the last of the three sections now.

Spend just a few minutes on this exercise.

The extract is from an interview and makes clear the devastating consequences for the local inhabitants. Equateur province was probably the scene of the worst atrocities, but atrocities also occurred elsewhere. Those directly killed by Free State soldiers and officials were probably a small part of the enormous loss of life in these years. Many died from starvation, forced migration, exhaustion and disease: the vast movement of peoples associated with the slave trade, the wars to suppress it and to conquer the Congo, and the implications of the rubber system, led to smallpox and sleeping sickness epidemics. Although no reliable figures are possible, some have suggested that the total death toll was as high as 10 million – half the population (Hochschild, 2002, ch. 15). Should this be seen as genocide? The question has recently been widely discussed in Belgium (Maréchal, 2005). Unit 24 will discuss accusations of genocide in the context of another African colony, so bear this question in mind.

Summary

This section has looked at how the Congo was ruled and at the consequences for the local population. It has highlighted the way that natural resources were plundered for short-term profit and the devastating consequences for local people of this economic system. The next section will look at the development of the international campaign that was eventually to end the Free State regime.

DVD exercise

Before moving on to the next section, look at section 2 of DVD 3, which explores how some of the profits of the Congo were used in Belgium. You will find further information about the DVD in the *Media Guide*.

Spend, at most, 2 hours on this exercise.

THE CAMPAIGN AGAINST LEOPOLD'S RULE IN THE CONGO

The beginnings of protest in Europe

As early as 1890, information about the brutality of the Free State regime began to reach Europe and the USA. The first reports often came from missionaries: Protestant mission groups from Britain, America and northern Europe established mission stations in the Congo basin at much the same time as the Free State and the concessionary companies were establishing trading posts. In some cases they preceded the Free State officials, in others they followed them – in all cases they inevitably came into contact with each other as the only westerners in the area. Missionaries were therefore in a better position to observe the activities of the Free State and company officials than any other Europeans. Through the missionary societies that had sent them, they also possessed the networks to convey reports back home.

One might indeed ask why reports did not emerge earlier. A number of factors played a part: the worst brutality often took place where there were no missionaries to witness it; it was not always easy for missionaries to report home; a reluctance to complicate relations with the civil authorities, which might lead to expulsion; their dependence on the Free State for security and transport; expectations about how European soldiers and officials would behave, particularly in the first phase of empire building (Grant, 2005, pp. 44–7). But it was not only a question of what news came from the Congo; it was also a question of how it was received. How did the European press report events?

EXERCISE

I would like you to explore this issue by searching for contemporary reports about atrocities in the Congo in *The Times*. Because many missionaries were British or worked for British missionary groups, and because Britain had extensive interests in Africa, Britain was one of the first countries where reports about conditions in the Free State emerged. It was in Britain, too, that the campaign against the regime first got off the ground. *The Times* is an excellent paper to explore such reports, since, in this period, it was widely seen as authoritative, and it had extensive links throughout Britain's governing circles. To the extent that any paper can be seen as speaking for a social group, *The Times* in this period was the voice of Britain's elite. Since *The Times* is available to you online through the OU Library, it is possible for you to conduct a search for primary material. How then did *The Times* report news from the Congo? And how did this change over time?

You will find some instructions for searching online on the course website. Please turn to these now.

Spend about 1–2 hours on this exercise.

DISCUSSION

I hope your search was successful and that you found some interesting texts. Since you are conducting the search, I cannot know what articles you identified nor what conclusions can be drawn from them. However, I think you will have found quite a sharp distinction between the 'news' articles, which often quote sources at length with little comment, and the letters to the editor, which make for lively reading. The letters include sharp exchanges between those supporting the Congo Free State (who are often revealed as officials of the Free State or of Belgium) and their opponents, who are sometimes writing on behalf of the Anti-Slavery Society or similar humanitarian organisations.

Perhaps the most interesting change over time is in the views expressed in *The Times* editorials. I picked out two which seemed to me to demonstrate this change. In a leader on 31 May 1897, *The Times* considers accusations by a Swedish missionary, Mr Sjöblom (described as Danish in the report). Although obviously disturbed by the accusations, the report is careful to weigh them against the answer by Col. Wahis, the governor-general of the Congo. If this answer is described as 'unsatisfactory', *The Times* argues that 'there is no conclusive evidence'. Note how in the second half of the long first paragraph, the nature of colonial rule (and African 'savage blood') are used to excuse excesses. My second report on 12 October 1903 takes a much harder line. The British government has sent a note about 'alleged misgovernment' in the Congo and the answers received so far are dismissed as 'weak and inconclusive' and later as 'vague and evasive'. Note how Leopold II is directly linked to the emerging scandal. He may 'rest assured that he will not hear the last' of the accusations until they are properly investigated.

The Congo campaign

Despite this hardening of public opinion against the Free State, the British government was reluctant to intervene in the internal affairs of another state. The official view was that, if there were atrocities, they were the work of individuals and that it was the responsibility of the Belgian government to control Leopold's regime. When a British trader was summarily executed by a

Free State officer in 1895 for supplying arms and ammunition to slave traders, the British government protested vigorously and insisted on compensation (Ewans, 2002, p. 180). But it was one thing to take action to protect British citizens, another to intervene on behalf of the African inhabitants of another colony. Remember, too, that this was the period of the Boer War when Britain was absorbed by other African concerns.

The protesters, however, argued that the terms of the Berlin Africa Conference Act gave Britain the right to intervene, and in 1903 the British government was persuaded to commission an investigation by the consul. Roger Casement's report, which appeared in 1904, made the extent of the atrocities public.

Roger Casement (1864–1916) was born into a Protestant Irish family and spent nearly twenty years in Africa, working first for shipping companies and later as a British consul. After writing his report on the Congo, he held various consular posts in Brazil, and wrote another devastating report on atrocities, this time in the Putamayo basin in Peru. He was knighted for his work, but came increasingly to support the Irish Nationalist cause. In 1914, he went to Germany, returning to Ireland in 1916 to support the Easter Rising. He was arrested almost immediately, tried for treason and executed in August 1916 (a profile of Casement can be found in the *Oxford Dictionary of National Biography*).

EXERCISE

You have already read a section of Casement's report in Anthology Document 6.14, 'Roger Casement's *Congo Report*, 11 December 1903'. Now read the whole extract.

Spend just a few minutes on this exercise.

Casement's report caused a sensation. For a sense of the impact, you might like to look again for reports in *The Times*. I picked up one for 8 June 1904, entitled 'The Congo Question' (there is a link to this article on the course website). It is a report of a public meeting attended by MPs and leading churchmen. The bishop of Hereford chaired the meeting, two leading Liberal MPs spoke, and the report starts with expressions of support from a long list of public figures. Calls were made for an international commission to investigate or for the Congo Free State to be dissolved.

Casement's report was itself the result of protests, and it was used by campaigners to keep up the pressure on the British government. Two strands in this protest movement can be identified, one developing from missionary circles, and one starting from a more radical perspective and associated in particular with the campaigning journalist E. D. Morel. There was cooperation between the two groups, but differences between them also existed. Let us first look at the activities of the missionary groups.

EXERCISE

Look at the *Visual Sources*, Plates 23.2 to 23.4, and consider the impact such photos might have. As in Unit 22, you may find it useful to think about their composition.

Spend about 10–15 minutes on this exercise.

SPECIMEN ANSWER

All three of the photos are shocking. The first shows two boys who have both lost a hand; the other two display severed limbs. All three photos are clearly arranged. In Plate 23.2, the white clothes worn by the boys form a background which effectively highlights the mutilated limbs. In Plate 23.3, it is the man's gaze that focuses attention on the severed hand and foot. In Plate 23.4, the presence of the white missionaries frames the photo, presumably to add to the authority of the image.

DISCUSSION

All the photos claim to show atrocities committed by soldiers or officials of the Congo Free State or the concessionary companies. Such photos were designed and used to demonstrate the brutality of the Congo regime (see Ryan 1997, pp. 222–4; Grant, 2005). The photograph in Plate 23.2 was taken in 1903 by Rev. W. D. Armstrong, a British missionary; the other two in the following year by Alice Harris (see Figure 23.4) who worked for the same mission group. The two white men in Plate 23.4 are her husband, Rev. John Harris, and their colleague, Rev. Edgar Stannard. Sending the photo in Plate 23.3 to the head of their mission, John Harris explained that it showed a father with all he had rescued of his young daughter's body after she had been killed and eaten by 'sentries' working for ABIR. Harris wrote 'the photograph is most telling, and as a slide will rouse any audience to an outburst of rage, the expression on the father's face, the horror of the by-standers the mute appeal of the hand and foot will speak to the most skeptical' (quoted in Grant, 2005, p. 40).

From the early 1900s on, returned missionaries and other evangelical speakers toured Britain speaking in church and civic halls and campaigning for British intervention in the Congo. Photos such as the ones shown here were a key part of hour-long 'lantern-slide lectures' built around the themes of promise (the purpose of the Free State), betrayal (the present atrocities) and redemption (the role of the missionaries). When Casement travelled to the Equateur province, he stayed with British missionaries who arranged meetings for him with Africans who had suffered at the hands of Free State officials. In turn, his report fuelled their campaign. In 1906–07, John and Alice Harris, now back from the Congo, gave over 300 talks, sometimes to audiences of 1,000 or more (Grant, 2005, pp. 66–74). Severed hands became one the most telling images in the fight for reform in the Congo (see Figures 23.5 and 23.6 for how the image crops up in cartoons about the Congo).

Why were such photos so widely used? Obviously, the mutilated body has the power to shock. Pictures of mute Africans appealing for help played on pity and drew on powerful traditions dating back to the abolitionists. But another reason why they were so effective was the widespread belief that photographs told the truth. Images – unlike words – do not lie.

The power of photographic evidence was recognised by supporters of Leopold II, who devoted considerable effort to undermining the veracity of the images. In an official answer to Casement's report, for instance, it was claimed for one

Figure 23.4 Photographer unknown, Alice Harris with a large group of Congolese children, early 1900s, lantern slide. Photo: Anti-Slavery International / Alice Harris

THE APPEAL.

"IN THE NAME OF ALMIGHTY GOD.—All the Powers exercising sovereign rights, or having influence in the said territories undertake to watch over the preservation of the native races, and the amelioration of the moral and material conditions of their existence."

Article VI. The Act of Berlin. 1885.

Figure 23.5   'The appeal', cartoon. An African with a severed hand appeals to John Bull for help against Leopold II (recognisable in the background). The African is holding a sheet of paper saying 'Act of Berlin 1885'. Reformers argued that the Act gave other powers the right and duty to intervene in the Congo. From Hochschild, 2002, source unknown

photo similar to Plate 23.2 that the boy's hand had been bitten off by a boar (Grant, 2005, p. 68; Ewens 2002, p. 207). Since Europeans rarely witnessed such incidents and many of them had only a limited grasp of Congolese languages and so relied on translators, there was room for uncertainty as to what actually had occurred. All three photos, after all, show the consequences of brutality rather than the actual events. Moreover, in one sense, the symbolic power of such images was based on a misrepresentation. Severing limbs was not a punishment authorised by the Free State (although some officers required their soldiers to cut the hands off corpses to prove that they had used their ammunition effectively); as such it could be dismissed as the excesses of African soldiers or lowly officials.

Les crimes coloniaux

LA COMMISSION D'ENQUÊTE AU CONGO

Extrait du rapport : Nous avons interrogé deux vic-
times qui avaient complètement perdu la tête et ne
savaient plus nous dire ce qui leur étaient arrivé.

Figure 23.6   'Les Crimes Coloniaux: La Commission d'Enquête au Congo', cartoon. Photo: Rex Features / Roger Viollet.
The cartoon is titled 'Colonial crimes. The Commission of the Inquiry in the Congo'. The text below the cartoon reads:
'Extract from the report: we interrogated two victims who had completely lost their heads and were quite unable to tell
us what happened'.

> **Edmund Dene Morel** (1873–1924) first became interested in the Congo when working as a clerk for a Liverpool shipping company that traded with the Free State. Increasingly active as a campaigning journalist, in 1903 he founded the *West African Mail* and in 1904, the Congo Reform Association. He became a full-time activist, first on the Congo issue, later against secret diplomacy and the First World War, which led briefly to his imprisonment. In 1918, he joined the Labour Party and became a foreign affairs spokesman. In 1922, he was elected to parliament for Dundee (after defeating Churchill). Again, Morel can be found in the *Oxford Dictionary of National Biography*.

Let us turn now to the other strand of the agitation. On his return from Africa in 1904, Casement persuaded Morel to form the Congo Reform Association, which came to lead the protests. By this point, Morel was already one of the most vociferous critics of Leopold's regime. Anthology Document 6.13 is an extract from E. D. Morel's *The Congo Slave State*, published in 1903. The first paragraphs in the extract analyse the process by which Leopold legally appropriated all land that was of commercial value in the Congo (you will recall that the products that Europeans wanted, such as ivory and rubber, were not the result of cultivation but were found in the wild) and then forced the local population to work for them by levying a tax in kind. The result was a system of forced labour: part of the sub-title of the pamphlet is *A Protest against the new African Slavery*. Do read the whole extract if you are interested, although in the exercise below you only need to read the final paragraph.

EXERCISE

Read the final paragraph of Anthology Document 6.13, 'Protests against atrocities in the Congo'. How does Morel's case in this paragraph compare with that made by the missionaries? Think about his language, his target and how he writes about African people.

Spend about 30 minutes on this exercise.

SPECIMEN ANSWER

In this text, Morel, like the missionaries, uses emotive language and associations to make his point. The sub-title of his pamphlet, for instance, explicitly links the labour practices of the Congo Free State to the slave trade it had been set up to eradicate. Morel may concentrate on economic arguments, but his message is also a moral one: what the Free State is doing is wrong. His focus, however, is not so much on abuses by agents of the state as on the system itself. His attack is indeed on Leopold himself (higher up in the text 'one man sitting in Brussels' is printed in bold). How Morel presents the African inhabitants of the Congo is also slightly different. While for him, too, they are victims, what he wants is for them to be allowed to be agents of their own fate. The phrase 'not a brute, but a man' is a striking one. While missionaries also stressed common humanity, the point that Morel was making was one not universally accepted in this period: that Africans would respond in the same way as Europeans to economic stimuli – if opportunities for trade or profit existed, Africans would take them.

Morel's focus on how profits were made in the Free State was influenced by the emerging critique of the economic roots of imperialism that you have encountered in Unit 21 when you looked at the writings of Hobson. Whereas a major goal of the missionary critics of the Congo Free State was greater opportunity for their missions, and their protests were partly influenced by the bias that the Free State showed to Belgian Catholic missionaries (Grant, 2005, pp. 46–7), Morel saw the salvation of Africa in free trade. Neither group was therefore arguing for a disengagement from Africa – Morel used the decisions of the Berlin Africa Conference to attack Leopold, and his position was closer to some of the participants in the Dundee debate about free trade and tariffs. Such a position was, of course, attractive to the Liverpool commercial circles where Morel started his career.

There were, therefore, important differences between the two wings of the campaign and they did not always find it easy to work together. Morel confided to an ally 'talk of religion in a matter of this kind sets my teeth on edge' (Grant, 2005, p. 62). Morel's command of the evidence (he was supremely well informed on the Congo Free State) and links in influential circles made him a powerful campaigner. But, as he recognised, the missionary networks were able to mobilise support on a far larger scale. It was the cooperation of the two groups that made the Congo Reform Association so effective.

International pressure on Leopold II and Belgium

So far, we have discussed the response in Britain. The campaign for reform was biggest in Britain, but there were always voices protesting against the policies of the Free State in other countries, including Belgium. Indeed, two of the most persistent critics of Leopold's regime were Félicien Cattier, a professor at the Free University of Brussels, and Emile Vandervelde, the leader of the Belgian Socialist Party. However, the very strength of the protest movement in Britain led many Belgians to side with Leopold. This was, after all, the period after the Boer War, when many Belgians (and people in other European countries) had supported the Boers against what they saw as arrogant British imperialists. It was easy for supporters of the Free State to paint Morel, in particular, as the agent of 'the Liverpool merchants' – British commercial interests seeking to fabricate a pretext for a British takeover of the Congo (Stengers, 1968).

The reception of Casement's report, however, made it harder for Leopold and his officials to ignore the continuing claims of atrocities. In response, they decided to send their own commission of inquiry to the Congo. This may have been an attempt to delay change or to demonstrate that action was being taken to correct the misdemeanours of minor officials; if, however, it was meant as a whitewash, it was spectacularly unsuccessful. Even though the three judges had been carefully selected, their cautiously phrased report, which was delivered in November 1905, was damning. By 1906, many Belgians were coming to realise that reports from the Congo were damaging the reputation of their country (Hochschild, 2002, pp. 250–1).

If the Congo Free State was to be abolished, how was the colony to be ruled instead? To most Europeans, no solution other than an imperial one was conceivable at the time. It was widely agreed that the best solution was for Belgium to take over the administration of the colony (see *The Times* report of June 1904 quoted above). In 1907, the Belgian parliament called on the government to negotiate the takeover the colony. As you know from Leopold's speeches, he claimed to have always wanted the colony to benefit Belgium; at the same time, he was determined to get as much compensation as possible for what he regarded as his assets. The negotiations were difficult and only in November 1908 was the Congo Free State formally dissolved. A year later, Leopold II was dead.

Morel and many British reformers doubted that Belgian rule would make much difference to the Congo, particularly since most of the officials stayed in post. As we have seen, however, the rubber boom, which had fuelled the worst excesses, was over by 1908, and tighter control from the centre also seems to have played a role in reducing the level of violence. What changed things most, however, was the First World War. Any Belgian doubts about colonial rule were forgotten as the colony became a major contributor to the war effort. After the war, Belgium exploited the colony's mineral resources and invested in its infrastructure. In 1914, too, British suspicions of Belgium were forgotten as it became 'plucky little Belgium' and the new king, Albert I, was lionised for his role in organising resistance to the Germans.

CONCLUSION

This unit starts with the Berlin Africa Conference and the considerations that led Bismarck to acquire colonies for Germany, and finishes with the exploitation of the Congo and the resulting atrocities. Unit 21 showed how hard it was to pinpoint the causes of the 'new imperialism' of the late nineteenth century. Is it easier in this case? Is it possible to draw a direct link between the Berlin conference and events in the Congo?

Let me finish with two assessments of the importance of the Berlin Africa Conference, both from the same collection of essays commemorating its 100th anniversary. The first is from a leading Nigerian historian, G. N. Uzoigwe. For him, 'the Berlin West Africa Conference is a landmark in world history. Never before, in the history of mankind, had a concert of one continent gathered together to plan how to share out another continent without the knowledge of the latter's leaders' (Uzoigwe, 1988, p. 541). The focus of his article, however, is on the consequences of the conference. The European powers agreed rules for dividing Africa and the rules proved effective: despite various scares, there were no wars between European states about partition and, indeed, the colonial frontiers drawn in the next decades have largely survived to this day. Equally important, the Berlin Act opened Africa to Christian missionaries and western education, and made it economically dependent on Europe. For Uzoigwe, 'the post-1885 history of Africa is, broadly speaking, a legacy of the Berlin West Africa Conference' (Uzoigwe, 1988, p. 552).

The second assessment is from H. L. Wesseling, a Dutch historian and one of the leading European experts on imperialism. Wesseling argues that the proceedings of the conference were of no great interest to the participants. He points out, for instance, that Bismarck barely attended, only turning up to open and close the conference (so much for Figure 23.1!), and does not mention it in his memoirs (Wesseling, 1988, pp. 528, 531). Many of the decisions were either of marginal significance or were later ignored (for instance, free trade in the Congo). Wesseling suggests, half tongue-in-cheek, 'we might even agree that the Conference was not such an important thing after all ... not a major event in world history or in the history of Africa' (p. 532). The importance of the conference, he argues, was largely symbolic. As the cartoon in Figure 23.2 shows (and similar ones appeared all over Europe), it was seen at the time as, and has come since to represent, the partition of Africa. Wesseling accepts that symbols are important and that colonial occupation was traumatic. At the same time, he cautions against linking too much subsequent history to the partition of the 1880s and 1890s. One reason why the division of Africa (as represented in maps such as Plate 23.1 in the *Visual Sources*) did not generate more conflict is that 'during the heyday of partition very little happened in Africa. What the maps illustrate is not reality but fiction. They illustrate the agreement on boundaries ... not the occupation itself. This came later' (p. 536).

How did these two historians reach such contrasting assessments of the Berlin Africa Conference? The explanation must surely partly be down to different perspectives – it is perhaps to be expected that historians writing in Europe and Africa do not see the process of partition in the same way. They also develop the question differently. Whereas Uzoigwe places the conference in a wide context, Wesseling analyses the actual events of 1884/85. As you have seen in previous units, the imperialism of the late nineteenth century has been much debated and many of the differences relate to the relationship between motives and outcomes or between specific events and wider contexts. As Wesseling writes, history is not like mechanics, where 'one can indicate the first shock – all that follows is predictable and can be traced back to it' (p. 534). We should be neither surprised nor dismayed to find that historians differ in their analyses.

REFERENCES

Ascherson, N. (1999 [1963]) *The King Incorporated. Leopold the Second and the Congo*, London, Granta.

Berghahn, V. (1994) *Imperial Germany, 1871–1918. Economy, Society, Culture and Politics*, Providence/Oxford, Berghahn Books.

Canis, K. (2002) 'Bismarck als Kolonialpolitiker', in Heyden, U. van der, and Zeller, J. (eds) *Kolonialmetropole Berlin. Eine Spurensuche*, Berlin, Berlin Edition.

Emerson, B. (1979) *Leopold II of the Belgians. King of Colonialism*, London, Weidenfeld & Nicolson.

Ewans, M. (2002) *European Atrocity, African Catastrophe. Leopold II, the Congo Free State and its Aftermath*, London, Routledge Curzon.

Förster, S., Mommsen, W.J. and Robinson, R. (eds) (1988) *Bismarck, Europe and Africa. The Berlin Africa Conference 1884–1885 and the Onset of Partition*, London, German Historical Institute and Oxford University Press.

Fröhlich, M. (1994) *Imperialismus. Deutsche Kolonial-und Weltpolitik 1880–1914*, Munich, dtv.

Grant, K. (2005) *A Civilised Savagery. Britain and the New Slaveries in Africa, 1884–1926*, New York, Routledge.

Harms, R. (1975) 'The end of red rubber: A reassessment', *Journal of African History*, vol. 16, pp. 73–88.

Harms, R. (1983) 'The World ABIR made: the Maringa-Lopori Basin, 1885–1903', *African Economic History*, vol. 12, pp. 125–39.

Hildebrand, K. (1989) *Deutsche Aussenpolitik 1871–1918*, Enzyklopädie Deutscher Geschichte, vol. 2, Munich, Oldenbourg.

Hochschild, A. (2002[1998]) *King Leopold's Ghost. A Story of Greed, Terror and Heroism in Colonial Africa*, London, Pan.

Kennedy, P.M. (1980) *The Rise of the Anglo-German Antagonism 1860–1914*, London, George Allan & Unwin.

Lambert, E. (1999) 'Belgium since 1830' in Blom, J.C.H and Lamberts, E. (eds) *History of the Low Countries*, Oxford, Berghahn.

Maréchal, P. (2005) 'La controverse sur Léopold II et le Congo dans la literature et les medias. Réflexions critiques' in *La mémoire du Congo. Le temps colonial*, Brussels, Editions Snoek.

Nelson, S. (1994) *Colonialism in the Congo Basin, 1880–1940*, Athens, Ohio, Ohio University Center for International Studies.

Osborn, E.L. (2004) '"Rubber fever", commerce and French colonial rule in Upper Guinée', *Journal of African History*, vol. 45, pp. 445–65.

Peemans, J.-P. (1975) 'Capital accumulation in the Congo under colonialism: the role of the state' in Duignan, P. and Gann, L.H (eds) *Colonialism in Africa*, vol. 4, *The Economics of Colonialism*, Cambridge, Cambridge University Press.

Robinson, R. (1988) 'The conference in Berlin and the future in Africa, 1884–1885' in Förster, Mommsen and Robinson (1988), pp.1–31.

Ryan, J.R. (1997) *Picturing Empire: Photography and the Visualization of the British Empire*, London. Reaktion.

Stengers, J. (1968) 'Morel and Belgium' in Louis, W.R. and Stengers, J. (eds) *E. D. Morel's History of the Congo Reform Movement*, Oxford, Clarendon Press.

Stengers, J. and Vansina, J. (1985) 'King Leopold's Congo, 1886–1908' in Oliver, R. and Sanderson, G.N. (eds) *The Cambridge History of Africa*, vol. 6, *From 1870 to 1905*, Cambridge, Cambridge University Press.

Uzoigwe, G.N. (1988) 'The results of the Berlin West Africa conference: an assessment', in Förster, Mommsen and Robinson (1988), pp. 541–52.

Vangroenweghe, D. (1986) *Du Sang sur les Lianes*, Brussels, Didier Hatier.

Wesseling, H.L. (1988) 'The Berlin conference and the expansion of Europe: a conclusion', in Förster, Mommsen and Robinson (1988), pp. 527–40.

Annika Mombauer, with Donna Loftus and Robin Mackie

INTRODUCTION

This unit continues our investigation of imperial Germany's colonial period, focusing on the development of German imperialism after the accession to power of Kaiser Wilhelm II in 1888. As we have explored, late nineteenth-century imperialism was the result of a complex mix of geopolitical, economic and social factors fuelled by increasing competition between the imperial powers. This unit further explores the interplay between domestic and foreign concerns that shaped policy in one of the most important and most aggressive imperial powers of the period: Germany. It also looks at the way that colonial 'possessions' were regarded and represented in Germany and how this influenced German responses to developments in the Far East and in Africa. As such, the unit relates most strongly to the themes of state formation and beliefs and ideologies. In addition, although the focus is still on European attitudes and actions, you will encounter some examples of resistance to imperial rule. The unit will consider two cases where protest at European expansion ended in conflict. As elsewhere in the block, however, the focus will be on the German response to this resistance, rather than on the resistance movements themselves. The unit will finish by looking at a debate between historians concerning German rule in South-West Africa: did Germans commit a genocide against Africans, long before the attempted genocide of the Jews in the Third Reich?

GERMANY DEMANDS ITS 'PLACE IN THE SUN': *WELTPOLITIK* UNDER WILHELM II

In Unit 23, we looked at Germany's initial period of colonial expansion under Bismarck in 1884–85. You will recall that historians have debated why Bismarck was suddenly keen to acquire colonies and the concept of 'social imperialism': that the drive for empire was motivated by internal considerations and, in particular, concerns about the political stability of a rapidly changing Germany. However, you will also remember that, whatever Bismarck's reasons for acquiring colonies, they were short term. After a brief spurt of empire building, Bismarck rapidly lost interest in Germany's new African and Pacific colonies.

Wilhelm II (1859–1941) became emperor (*Kaiser*) of Germany and king of Prussia in 1888, following the death of his father, Frederick, who had only ruled for 3 months. Through his mother, Wilhelm II was the grandson of Queen Victoria. Shortly after acceding to the throne, in 1890, he dismissed the long-serving German chancellor Otto von Bismarck, and thereafter played a prominent, if unpredictable, role in German public affairs and particularly in foreign and military policy. Wilhelm remained emperor throughout the First World War, but was forced to abdicate in 1918, as a condition for peace. He fled Germany for the Netherlands, living there in exile until his death.

In 1888, a new emperor, Kaiser Wilhelm II, acceded to the throne of Germany. We have seen in Unit 21 (and indeed in Unit 22 when discussing tariff reform) that one facet of the debate about the causes of British imperialism relates to how government decisions were made and the amount of influence that different groups wielded. Germany also had a parliament (*Reichstag*) in which opposition parties were represented, and, as was discussed in Unit 23, there were also many, vociferous imperialist pressure groups. However, the system of government in Germany gave the Kaiser considerable power if he chose to use it, particularly through his right to appoint the chancellor. Wilhelm II was keen to play a far more active role in policy making and was quick to undo Bismarck's relatively restrained foreign policy both in Europe and worldwide. Bismarck was dismissed in 1890 and his successors as chancellor never enjoyed such complete control over foreign policy. In Europe, Bismarck's carefully constructed alliance system, designed to prevent the emergence of an anti-German coalition, was allowed to crumble. Germany entered a new era, in which its rapid development was to be reflected in the achievement of the status of a world power. This goal was summarised in a phrase coined by the foreign secretary Bernhard von Bülow (who was later to become chancellor) in December 1897. On the occasion of the German occupation of the Chinese port of Kiaochow, Bülow declared to the *Reichstag*: 'We are very willing to take into consideration the interests of other great powers in East Asia, providing that our own interests also find adequate consideration by them. In one word: We don't want to put anyone in the shade, but we demand our place in the sun too' (quoted in Bruch and Hofmeister, 2000, p. 270).

As was the case in Britain, one aspect of a more active imperial policy was popular interest. Many Germans felt that Germany had missed out when other European nations had acquired their imperial possessions. Germany's large population and its economic success were also seen as reasons why Germany needed and deserved an empire. Since unification in 1871, Germany had caught up and overtaken most of its major competitors in terms of industrial output, and by the early twentieth century Germany had emerged as the strongest economic power on the continent of Europe. One measure of economic prowess widely used at the time was the production of iron, the material used in many nineteenth-century industrial products. Table 24.1 gives figures for iron production in the major European states.

Table 24.1   Pig iron production in Germany, Britain, France and Russia, in annual averages, 1870–1913 ('000s)

Year	Germany	Britain	France	Russia
1870–74	1,579	6,480	1,211	375
1875–79	1,770	6,484	1,462	424
1880–84	2,893	8,295	1,918	477
1885–89	3,541	7,784	1,626	616
1890–94	4,335	7,402	1,998	1,096
1895–99	5,974	8,777	2,386	1,981
1900–04	7,925	8,778	2,665	2,773
1905–09	10,666	9,855	3,391	2,779
1910–13	14,836	9,792	4,664	3,870

(Source: Berghahn, 1994, p. 298)

EXERCISE

Take a few moments to look at the figures in Table 24.1 and summarise what they reveal about German production. How well do they support the case for imperial expansion?

Spend about 5–10 minutes on this exercise.

SPECIMEN ANSWER

In 1870–74, Germany produced only a quarter as much iron as Britain and was only slightly ahead of France. By 1900–04, it had almost drawn level with Britain and by 1910–13, it produced over 50 per cent more than Britain and more than three times as much as France.

The table does not really make a case for empire. Germany's iron production was already growing rapidly before colonies were acquired and the acquisition of colonies in 1884–85 made no difference to the rate of increase. If there had been a clear link between industrial expansion and empire, one would have expected Britain, France and Russia, which all had far larger empires, to show higher growth rates.

DISCUSSION

As you know from the previous units, the economic case for empire was much debated at the time. However, even if the need for colonies was open to question, it is perhaps not surprising that the rulers of the new, powerful Germany wanted to see their economic prestige and political interests reflected abroad. The term *Weltpolitik* (literally, 'world policy') was used to refer both to Germany's foreign policy in Europe under Wilhelm II, and to its wish for expansion of German influence worldwide. Just as production figures might be used as a proxy measure of national strength, so too did the possession of colonies and spheres of influence come to be seen as representing global power. We have seen in Unit 21 how some British political leaders saw the empire as both evidence of British superiority and a means to maintaining British pre-eminence. Such ideas were also current in Germany, and Britain was envied for its large empire. Many Germans felt that in order for Germany to become a world power, with a status commensurate with its highly developed industry, large population and wealth, it must also acquire protectorates in Africa, Asia and the Pacific.

The chronology in the *Course Guide* provides you with an overview of the major events in German colonial expansion in this period. The period after 1890 saw some further expansion, although the territorial gains were often relatively unimportant. Germany had only limited bargaining power, particularly with the British. For example, the Heligoland–Zanzibar Treaty of 1890, an Anglo-German colonial treaty, settled various disputes over territory in East, West and South-West Africa. Germany was given the North Sea island of Heligoland (which remains German to this day), and access to the Zambezi river through the so-called Caprivi Strip. But Germany had to give up its hope of establishing a protectorate over Zanzibar and to give up Uganda to Britain. The explorer Carl Peters, who had founded the Gesellschaft für deutsche Kolonisation (Corporation for German Colonisation), which became the Deutsch-Ostafrikanische Gesellschaft (German East-Africa Company) in 1885, summed up this unfavourable deal by stating that Germany had 'exchanged three kingdoms for a bathtub' (quoted in Wirtz, 1982, p. 391).

Moreover, these relatively limited gains led to conflict and rivalries, particularly with Britain. The heightening tension resulted in a number of international crises (some of these are listed in your chronology). These included a conflict over the Samoan islands in 1893, over central and south Africa in 1894, the Jameson Raid in the Transvaal, the agreement over Portuguese colonial possessions, and the conflict with the USA over Manila in 1898, among others. Don't worry, you won't need to memorise these, as long as you are aware of the fact that Germany clashed frequently on colonial issues with the other great powers as it attempted to assert its imperial claims. In 1897, Germany acquired the Chinese port of Kiaochow, and in 1901, Germany conquered and occupied North Cameroon, adding to its territorial possessions in Africa. By the time the First World War broke out, Germany possessed the territories listed in Table 24.2.

One of the domestic consequences of Germany's continuing expansion was a new focus on building a navy, in a country where the emphasis had always been on the army. In the 1897 speech in which he demanded a 'place in the sun', Bülow also stressed the importance of developing German shipping, trade and industry. The needs of industry and commerce were frequently used as arguments in favour of German colonial expansion: it was maintained that Germany needed access to new export markets, markets that were seemingly within easy reach. This was linked to the vast new fleet-building programme that Germany embarked on from 1897. The huge expense of this expansion was justified by the need for a powerful fleet to supply and police Germany's colonial territories. In reality, many of the large ships that were built under the building programme of Admiral Alfred von Tirpitz were not capable of travelling to Germany's far-flung colonies, but were largely designed for naval battle in the North Sea – that is, to fight the British navy at some future point. However, in terms of propaganda at home, the colonies served as justification for the vast expenditure on capital (i.e. large) ships. It would have been impossible to rally the *Reichstag* (whose budgetary powers meant that it could veto any large expenditure on naval building) with a cry for a 'fleet against England'.

Table 24.2   German colonial territories and population sizes in 1914

	Area (1000 km^2)	Native inhabitants ('000s)	White inhabitants ('000s)
Africa			
Togo	88	1,031	0.4
Cameroon	504	3,326	1.8
German South-West Africa	830	80	15
German East Africa	1,020	7,645	5
Asia and Pacific Ocean			
Palau, Caroline, Marianne and Marshall Islands	13.2	15	0.5
Samoa	25.5	35	0.5
German New Guinea and Bismarck Archipelago	230	719	0.9
Kiaochow	0.56	192	4.4

(Source: Bruch and Hofmeister, 2000, pp. 260–1)

From the late 1890s onwards, therefore, Germany was gripped by both a naval and a colonial fever, and the government was able to utilise public opinion to achieve support for its foreign expansion, while simultaneously building a new German navy which might, in time, be used to threaten British naval supremacy. With their passionate rhetoric and propaganda, colonial expansion and fleet building were always partly about creating national cohesion and domestic unity. Although, as we saw in Unit 21, it is hard to decide how significant a factor public opinion was, or indeed how much consensus there was on these issues, there seems little doubt that Germany's rulers encouraged and exploited popular support for imperial expansion in a bid to underpin its domestic power – very much in the way the historians who talk about 'social imperialism' suggest. Despite the emphasis on the economic benefits of expansion in imperialist rhetoric, the colonies' economic importance, though not completely negligible, was by no means the major factor behind Germany's drive towards empire.

REPRESENTATIONS OF EMPIRE IN THE GERMAN REICH

As in Britain, empire and colonialism permeated German culture and society in the late nineteenth century as colonial products, images and artefacts became a part of everyday life. As you can see from Figures 24.1–24.3, empire shaped the urban landscape through buildings and commerce. *Kolonialwaren* (colonial

Figure 24.1 The Deutsches Kolonialhaus (German colonial house) in Berlin Lützowstrasse, built in 1903, from *Deutsche Kolonialzeitung*, 1903

wares), including coffee, chocolate, rubber and tobacco, were highly prized goods available in specialist shops and the object of much interest.

In addition, there were widespread exhibitions and public displays of the products and artefacts of empire to encourage trade and educate and entertain audiences. In 1899, Wilhelm II opened the *Kolonialmuseum* (colonial museum) in Berlin, which aimed to represent life in the colonies to the German public.

Its conception had been preceded by the first German Colonial Exhibition, which had been part of the 1896 Berlin Trade Fair (see Figure 24.4). In addition to this first major exhibition, others followed in a number of German cities, as well as exhibitions of African peoples in museums and zoos. *Völkerschauen* (peoples' exhibitions), the Colonial/Transvaal Exhibition of 1896/7, and the Samoa show in Berlin's zoo in 1900 are examples of this trend. As in the Brussels Exhibition of 1897 that you studied on DVD 3

Figure 24.2   The inside of the cigar room of the Deutsches Kolonialhaus (German colonial house) in Jerusalemer Strasse, from *Deutsche Kolonialzeitung*, 1901

section 2, Africans were exhibited in recreated villages, and drew crowds curious about their dress, customs, tools, houses and so on.

As you have already seen in earlier units, such exhibitions and spectacles were organised in many countries. Fascination with the 'exotic' nature of the native peoples was cultivated in the way they were represented to the public in Germany and elsewhere. As you saw in *The Times* report of the 'Greater Britain Exhibition', native peoples of the colonised lands were seen as curiosities to be observed, their habits and appearance strange and alien. In some cases, they were presented to the public with strange animals from distant lands; Africans were included in the exhibits of some of the large zoos in Germany. At the same time, pseudo-scientific notions of racial difference derived from social Darwinism and employing 'research' (such as craniology – the measuring of skulls) could be used to confirm ideas of German superiority and construct hierarchies of race. In addition, other 'inferior' races were often portrayed as dangerous or evil, as was the case with so-called 'yellow' races of

Figure 24.3   A group of African employees of the Deutsches Kolonialhaus, from *Deutsche Kolonialzeitung*, 1901

Asia, while the superiority of some (white) races and Christian religion (and the concomitant desire to export Christian beliefs into the 'heathen' communities of the colonies) was confirmed. Despite the pervasiveness of such ideas of race, the German state felt the need to police the boundaries of racial interaction. In fact, it did not take long for special legislation to be introduced to deal with the unwelcome effects of racial mixing. Mixed marriages were outlawed in Germany. *(although it doesn't say when)*

As you know from Unit 21, although historians have explored the ideas behind imperial culture, the relationship between ideas and policy usually remains quite difficult to understand. Plate 24.1 therefore provides an unusual example of how racist ideas framed the decisions made by leaders.

Figure 24.4 Performance of a dance from the Tonga contingent at the Deutsches Kolonialaustellung (German Colonial Exhibition) in Berlin in 1896, engraving after a drawing by Wilhelm Kuhnert. Photo BPK, Berlin

Study the drawing *Peoples of Europe Protect your Holiest Possessions* (*Völker Europas wahret Eure heiligsten Güter*) in the *Visual Sources*, Plate 24.1, which was completed by Hermann Knackfuß, a German art professor, on the basis of a sketch by Wilhelm II. Note what is depicted and analyse the way Asia is characterised.

Spend about 10–15 minutes on this exercise.

The drawing depicts a Europe threatened by the east. The European nations, shown as female characters, are being asked by an angel (it is St Michael) to defend Europe and Christianity (symbolised by the cross). In the east, dark clouds and a shadowy Buddha figure symbolise anti-Christian, dark and menacing Asia. The drawing depicts the struggle of the Occident (the west) versus the Orient (the east).

Wilhelm II sent this sketch as a gift to the Russian tsar in 1895. He described it thus: it showed 'the European powers [...] how they united to defend the cross in resistance against the intervention of Buddhism, Heathendom and Barbarism' (quoted in Röhl, 2001, p. 841). Here, however, in the character of Wilhelm, we have evidence of the idea he had formed of the west and the 'Orient', which probably informed his policy in the Far East. Also interesting here, despite growing European rivalry over territory and influence in Africa and Asia, is the suggestion of an emerging European identity formed in opposition to 'Orientals', presented here as a common enemy.

A European settler in German South-West Africa

Similar beliefs in the superiority of Europeans and disdain for the 'heathens' can also be found in contemporary accounts of life in the German colonies in Africa. Such sources also give us an impression of how Africans were portrayed in Germany at the time. The accounts of explorers and other travellers played an important part in constructing European 'knowledge' of Africa, which, in turn, shaped how European travellers and settlers understood their experience overseas.

The Anthology contains three extracts from one such text – the account by a German woman, Else Sonnenberg, and of her experience in South-West Africa in 1903–04. Her narrative provides a particularly vivid description of a European's encounter with Africa.

Turn to Anthology Document 6.16, 'German settlers and the Herero uprising, 1904', and read the first extract from Sonnenberg's book, extract (a) 'How the Herero lived'. As explained in the header note, Else Sonnenberg arrived in German South-West Africa (now Namibia) in March 1903 to join her husband, less than a year before a major rebellion by one of the African peoples of the colony, the Herero. You will learn more about her experience of the Herero rebellion later in the unit. Let us first look at her descriptions of the Herero people.

While reading the document, take notes and answer the following questions. In thinking about your answers, consider not only Sonnenberg's views, but also how her account might have been read in Germany.

1   How does Else Sonnenberg describe the Herero customs she discusses?

2   How would you characterise her opinion of the Herero?

3   What does Sonnenberg have to say about her relations with the Herero and German–Herero relations more generally?

Spend about 20–30 minutes on this exercise.

SPECIMEN ANSWER

1   In her description of everyday life in a Herero village, Sonnenberg highlights how different their lives were from those of Europeans. Her description of how they live, their marriage customs and their belief in spirits are all presented in a way that will have struck European readers as curious and alien. Very often she describes features so as to emphasise aspects that she feels are primitive and superstitious: the Herero have no concept of time, they believe things that Europeans know not to be true.

2   Although she does not use the word, she certainly considers the Herero to be primitive, and inferior to the European settlers. Her descriptions of their way of life, their customs, smells and foodstuffs are largely negative. Even when describing their homes in an apparently objective manner, she undermines this through the use of sarcasm ('the entire magnificent building'). She suggests they are lazy ('lives for the day without worry') and easily bought ('everyone is his master who gives him some tobacco'). She disapproves of their attitude towards marriage and their treatment of children (which is at the same time too lenient and yet too careless for her liking), and she is dismissive of their beliefs. She considers them to be thieves and does not condemn the extremely harsh punishment of the boy who took the chickens. Her more favourable comments are reserved for the Herero who have been baptised, but even this is qualified by the last sentence. There is nothing in this account that might leave readers with a favourable impression. Although Europeans had at times found much to admire in the way of life and attitudes of more 'natural' non-European peoples, there is certainly no hint of this here.

3   Sonnenberg has quite extensive contacts with the Herero ('daily dealings with the people and hundreds of them came to us'). Interestingly, she knows the Herero names for many items. At the same time, the relations are clearly not ones between equals; note for instance that the washer-woman has been given a German name. She also emphasises that, in her opinion, she went out of her way to be friendly towards the Herero and that she and her husband had good relations with them – there is the suggestion that not all Germans were as friendly (this becomes more explicit in later extracts). This adds to the dramatic impact of the final sentence.

Else Sonnenberg's account is a personal one, and was written after the Herero uprising (which will be discussed later in the unit), during which her husband was killed. As she suggests in the passage, her experience of the uprising led her to rethink her views. But this process of imagining the Herero started before she arrived in South-West Africa. Elsewhere in her book, Else Sonnenberg considers how her attitude towards the Herero changed once she arrived in the country:

*attitudes
to
"negroes"*

> While I lived among the Herero, I did not have a bad opinion of them
> on account of the fact that they were an uncultivated negro-tribe. In
> Germany I had imagined them much rawer and out of control,
> particularly vis-à-vis whites.
>
> (Sonnenberg, 1905, p. 32)

Her expectations had been shaped before she travelled to the colony; in turn,
her story will have helped form German attitudes to Africa. As such, the
opinions discussed here were significant in shaping and reinforcing negative
stereotypes. That her account was published in 1905 was almost certainly the
result of the uprising: events in South-West Africa created a demand in
Germany for information and stories from the colony. It is perhaps helpful to
think in terms of a circular process in which beliefs about Africa (or other
continents) helped shape how those who went overseas experienced the
colonies, while their experience and their reports in turn reaffirmed or modified
existing prejudices back home.

RESISTANCE TO COLONIAL RULE

Yet how Europeans thought about the non-European world was also shaped by
the peoples subjected to imperial invasion or conquest. In particular, resistance
to invasion or rebellions against colonial rule made a deep impression on
European consciousness. As you saw in Unit 21, ideas of racial difference
appeared to harden in the nineteenth century as a response to resistance to
British imperial rule. In the rest of this unit we will focus on two episodes
where resistance caused a particularly profound response in Germany. In the
first of two case studies, we will look at the rebellion in China in 1900, which
is known in Europe as the Boxer Rebellion. This investigation will highlight
common European opinions and prejudices against the 'yellow peril', and will
show how the European great powers attempted to overcome their deep
divisions in the face of a common enemy.

We will then return to Africa for the second case study, and look at the Herero
and Nama uprisings of 1904 in German South-West Africa. You will find out
about the underlying reasons for these revolts, and learn about the reaction of
the German colonial rulers to these events. The criticisms from some quarters
in Germany of the brutal suppression of these and other uprisings will also be
discussed.

The Boxer Rebellion

In the spring and summer of 1900, the colonial powers in China experienced a
violent backlash against their 'civilising' and missionary undertakings in the
country. By this time, Britain, France, Russia, Italy, Japan and Germany had
commercial interests in China and had carved up the country into different
'spheres of interest', while the USA had affirmed their own interests in east
Asia with their acquisition of the Philippines. By 1900, following a devastating
drought and in the light of widespread discontent at the way the colonial

powers treated the Chinese, a revolt by members of a secret society, the so-called Fists of Righteous Harmony, led thousands of Chinese to rise against the foreigners. The Europeans referred to this society as the 'Boxers', because of their practice of martial arts, and used this name to describe the uprising. The war against the Boxers resulted in an unusual cooperation between the western powers in the face of a perceived common enemy. Faced with an anti-imperial uprising, the European powers, together with Japan and the USA, worked together to suppress the rebellion. In 1900, this was still an option, as the European alliance system was not yet as rigid as it would be within a few years, when the divisions between the European powers led to war. Let us look in a little more detail at the events of 1900.

EXERCISE

An account of the Boxer Rebellion from the Prologue of *A Brief History of the Boxer Rebellion* by Diana Preston is available in the secondary sources on the course website – read this now. This will provide you with a good summary of the background and events of the rebellion and is a good introduction to the topic. Then summarise what she says about how Darwin's theory of evolution was used and the idea of the 'yellow peril'. You should also note your impression of what kind of a historical account you are reading. Who do you think it is written for?

Spend about 30–60 minutes on this exercise.

SPECIMEN ANSWER

Preston explains that Darwinism was used to 'legitimize distinctions between races and between individuals, and to justify the existence of social hierarchies'. She goes on to give examples of how this (mis-)interpretation of Darwinism (sometimes referred to as 'social Darwinism') was used to justify conquest and even the extermination of other peoples. One aspect of this racist thinking was fear of the 'yellow peril': that an armed and dangerous Asia was turning its gaze on Europe. Asians were represented as cruel and cunning and Darwinist theory was used to lend scientific credence to such beliefs, in which Oriental peoples were seen as 'less highly evolved and more prey to savage animal instincts'.

This text is slightly less 'academic' than some of the other secondary reading for the course. It is likely that it was written for a general audience, rather than for experts in the field.

DISCUSSION

Perhaps you also noted that Preston writes from an American/European perspective. She has made use of European accounts of the Boxer Rebellion, many of which were sensationalist and alarmist in tone, and, except in the final passage, has relatively little to say about how the Chinese viewed Europeans. The final quote, however, hints at the distance between European and Chinese views of the world.

Because of its trade in the region, German interests were affected by the rebellion, and German nationals were among those trapped inside the Chinese capital. That German troops would be involved in any international response to the atrocities was therefore probable. A significant German involvement became a certainty when news arrived in early July that the German envoy, Clemens von Ketteler, had been brutally murdered, leading the outraged Kaiser to demand revenge. In Wilhelm II's judgement, Germany now needed to play a significant role in whatever action would be decided upon.

Germany at this time was at the height of its fleet-building programme. Public opinion also favoured a German involvement in China, as Alfred von Waldersee, the general who was later put in charge of the German expeditionary army and of the international joint military forces, reported in a letter in August 1900: 'You cannot imagine the heightened mood at home. Something like this has not occurred since the outbreak of war [in 18]70; unfortunately it cannot stay this way and has to die down one day' (quoted in Mombauer, 2003, p. 94).

It is not surprising in the light of what is known of Wilhelm II's belligerent character that his reaction to the bloody events was one of outrage and indignation, and that he was spoiling for a fight. He claimed to have foreseen that such an event was likely to occur; had he not in fact predicted it in his infamous drawing sent to the tsar (see *Visual Sources*, Plate 24.1)? However, as so often in such situations during Wilhelm II's reign, there was more at stake than avenging the horrors inflicted on foreign victims, or the assassination of the German envoy in Peking, or even than staking a claim in China. Rather, Wilhelm wanted to demonstrate to the world that Germany was a power to be reckoned with, and he wanted to be seen to be playing an important role in international affairs. 'The ocean is indispensable for Germany's power. But the ocean also demonstrates that no important decisions must be taken on it, far from Germany, without Germany and without the German Kaiser,' he famously declared in a speech in July 1900 (Penzler, 1904, p. 208). Moreover, although Wilhelm and the German foreign office differed in their methods, both were anxious that other great powers, particularly Britain, but also Japan and Russia, should not use the current crisis to their advantage by extending their influence in the region. For all these reasons it was seen as essential that Germany be prominently involved in whatever action would be decided on by the powers.

For Wilhelm, the events themselves amounted to much more than a simple revolt in China. He considered it a fight between Asia and Europe, or between the Orient and the Occident (notwithstanding the fact that Japan fought on the side of the European powers, and that the USA was also involved). In this struggle, Wilhelm contended, the European powers had to be united if they were not to lose out to the 'yellow peril'. Although his response was certainly extreme, it should nonetheless be seen in the context of the general European outrage at the Boxer Rebellion. In their concern for the safety of the trapped Europeans in Peking, all the great powers hurriedly despatched troops to the region. It was even reported very confidentially that the pope might launch a crusade (Young, 1970, p. 149).

Wilhelm also evoked images of a medieval crusade. Some of his most notorious public speeches were made in response to the Boxer Rebellion. Most infamous of all was the 'Hun speech' in Bremerhaven on 27 July 1900, which is discussed below and which Bülow (then foreign secretary) considered 'perhaps the most damaging speech that Wilhelm II ever held' (Bülow, 1930, p. 359). His private and official correspondence of these months makes for equally shocking reading. As Thomas Nipperdey comments, 'the elaborate accompanying music and the new ideology of the "yellow peril" stood in no relation to the actual possibilities and results' (Nipperdey, 1994, p. 655). On 18 June, Wilhelm sent a telegram to Bülow, demanding 'exemplary punishment and preventive rules against repetition [of acts against European nationals]; i.e. armed intervention' (*Grosse Politik*, vol. 16, no. 4525, 1900, in Lepsius, Mendelsohn-Bartholdy and Thimme, 1922–27). According to Bülow's memoirs, in the summer of 1900, the Kaiser gave speeches 'which were intended to impress not just the Chinese, but the entire world' (Bülow, 1930, p. 358).

One of Wilhelm's major concerns was that Germany's rivals might use the situation to the detriment of Germany. He feared that other states, and in particular Russia or Japan, would use armed intervention to dominate proceedings in the Far East. For this reason, he was keen to send German naval and military troops to China. He also wanted a coordinated European effort which would revenge the 'grave embarrassment of the Europeans in front of Asians'. He demanded a 'grand military action of a uniform nature':

> Peking must actually be attacked and razed to the ground. For this the army must be equipped with quick firing artillery and with siege artillery. [...] I would gladly perhaps supply the commanding general. Then the entire undertaking must be placed in one firm hand, and a European one. We must never expose ourselves to a situation in which Russia and Japan sort the matter on their own and push Europe out. The German envoy will be revenged by my troops. Peking must be razed.
>
> (*Grosse Politik*, vol. 16, no. 4527, 1900, in Lepsius, Mendelsohn-Bartholdy and Thimme, 1922–27)

On his own authority, the Kaiser swiftly mobilised two battalions of navy infantry for despatch to China. In addition, a volunteer brigade, the East Asian Expeditionary Corps (*Ostasiatisches Expeditionskorps*), was formed under the leadership of Generalleutnant von Lessel. The Kaiser saw off the first of its contingents on 2 July. In contravention of the constitution, he failed to consult the *Reichstag* before ordering these measures, so bent was he on his 'campaign of vengeance' (*Rachefeldzug*). He did not even consider it necessary to run his policies past the chancellor. Wilhelm's speech on the troops' departure was of bombastic proportions:

> The torch of war has been thrown into the middle of the deepest peace, unfortunately not unexpected by me. A crime of unheard-of cheek, horrifying in its cruelty, has hit my trusted envoy and has killed him. [...] The German flag has been insulted and the German Reich has been humiliated. This demands exemplary punishment and vengeance. [...] Thus I send you out to avenge this injustice, and I shall not rest until German flags, united with those of the other

powers, fly victoriously above those of the Chinese and, placed upon
the walls of Peking, dictate the peace to them.

(Penzler, 1904, pp. 205–7)

Only in November, when German troops were already involved in fighting in
China, did Wilhelm address the *Reichstag*, justifying his actions with an appeal
to its members' patriotism and their outrage at the events in China. Many
parties were represented in the *Reichstag* and not all were persuaded by the
Kaiser's rhetoric. The Social Democrat leader August Bebel, who was opposed
to imperialist expansion, declared in a speech to the *Reichstag*:

> No, this is no crusade, no holy war; it is a very ordinary war of
> conquest [...]. A campaign of revenge as barbaric as it has never been
> seen in the last centuries, and not often at all in history; [...] not even
> with the Huns, not even with the Vandals [...]. That is no match for
> what the German and other troops of the foreign powers, together
> with the Japanese troops, have done in China.
>
> (Quoted in Felber and Rostek, 1987, p. 43)

Yet Germany's political system meant that such protests had little influence on
the policy of the government. At the other extreme, the Kaiser, in his speeches
and actions, retained a far greater ability to grab the agenda, even if, as we
have seen, government ministers such as Bülow were at times dismayed by his
views. Let us look in a little more detail at one of the most notorious of his
speeches.

The 'Hun speech'

There were many occasions in July and August 1900 when Wilhelm was able
to air his views about the Chinese, and about the task 'his' troops would have
to face in the Far East. Perhaps the most infamous occasion was his address to
the volunteers of the first regiment of the East Asian Expeditionary Corps on
27 July as they left from Bremerhaven for China – the so-called 'Hun speech',
since in it Wilhelm invoked the example of Attila and the Huns who invaded
Europe in the fifth century (see Figure 24.5).

EXERCISE

Read Anthology Document 6.15, 'The "Hun speech"', which is an extract from
Wilhelm II's speech, and comment on the language used and the impression this
speech would have made on contemporaries. You will notice some words in
parenthesis. How do you think these change the meaning of the text?

Spend about 15–30 minutes on this exercise.

SPECIMEN ANSWER

The language used in this speech is brutal. Germany's soldiers were instructed by
their monarch, to 'take no prisoners', and to defeat the Chinese in such a way that
no Chinese would 'ever dare so much as to look askance at a German'. The speech is
also very emotive and would probably have instilled a sense of patriotism in the
young men who were about to embark for China.

The words in parenthesis alter the meaning of that sentence (and arguably of the
speech) significantly. Did the Kaiser instruct his men not to grant any pardon to the

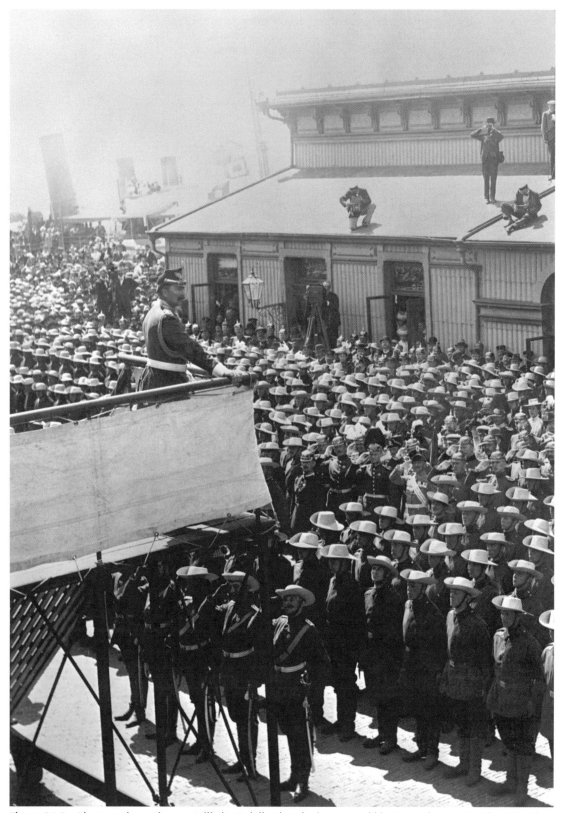

Figure 24.5   Photographer unknown, Wilhelm II delivering the 'Hun speech' in Bremerhaven, 27 July 1900. Photo: Bildarchiv, Zentrale Beschaffung Fotografie, Hamburg

Chinese and to be harsh to them, or did he warn them that the 'cunning enemy' would not be granting them any pardon? There is clearly a difference depending on which version of the sentence we use.

DISCUSSION

We do not actually know the exact wording of the speech. What we have are some slightly differing versions recorded by journalists who were present that day (you can see one of the reporters on the roof in the photograph!). Thus, we are not sure if Wilhelm II instructed the soldiers not to take any prisoners (which is how the line 'pardon will not be granted' is usually interpreted), or if he was telling them that the enemy would not take prisoners. However, it is clear that he urged his men to take revenge, and we know that this speech was widely deprecated both inside and outside Germany (see the French cartoon in Figure 24.6, for example).

— « On n'accordera aucun quartier; ouvrez son chemin à la civilisation une fois pour toutes. »

Figure 24.6   d'Hermann-Paul, 'Wilhelm II during the Boxer Rebellion', cartoon in *Le Cri de Paris*, 5 August 1900. From John Grand-Carteret, *Les célébrités vues par l'image 'Lui' devant l'objectif caricatural*, Paris, 1906, p.178. 'Pardon will not be granted; open a path for culture once and for all'

It is certainly true that the so-called 'Hun speech' was unique and nothing similar was said by the leaders of other powers who were involved in the Far East. Moreover, as Imanuel Geiss points out, it 'provided Allied propaganda with one of the most effective slogans to use against the German Empire during the First World War' (Geiss, 1976, p. 85). But other, less infamous speeches also deserve quoting, particularly as they reveal much about Wilhelm's attitude regarding the nature of the enemy that Germany and the allied troops were facing. On 2 August, in a farewell speech on the steamer *Rhein*, he declared: 'We are dealing with a cunning enemy who, if spared at one end, will emerge with deceit at the other. The Chinese [is] by nature cowardly like a dog, but also deceitful' (Penzler, 1904, p. 220). Similarly, in another farewell speech, the Kaiser was reported to have said to departing officers: 'Beware of underestimating the opponents. [...] Always imagine you [are] fighting an equal opponent. But don't forget his deceitfulness' (Penzler, 1904, pp. 221–3).

In fact, the campaign was to prove a disappointment to those most eager for war. Because of the size of the country, and the relatively limited numbers of allied troops, it was difficult to coordinate a campaign involving the different international armies or engage in large-scale battles. German officers were also disappointed by the nature of the enemy who, informed of the allies' actions by good communications, usually managed to avoid a confrontation. In the eyes of the German military, the enemy 'lacked an energetic will to fight' and did not fight according to the rules. For this reason, and also because of the difficulties imposed on the allied troops by the terrain, it was impossible to achieve 'overwhelming military successes, measured against European examples' (Mohs, 1929, p. 411). The Kaiser steadily lost interest in the campaign in the Far East following the liberation of the foreign nationals in Peking in August 1900, and, only a few months later, despite his earlier belligerence, he did not want to hear anything more about the matter.

The Germans soon also realised the limitations of the attempt at international cooperation in China. General Waldersee complained frequently about the distrust and even hatred that existed between the allied contingents, and about their differing, and often opposing, aims. In November, he commented in his diary on the difficult peace negotiations: 'The interests of the European powers are totally different and an honest collaboration is completely out of the question. If an understanding is reached in an area, then in reality nobody actually trusts the other one.' A few days later he wrote: 'Russian and English officers have sometimes been close to shooting at each other. The English, Russians, French each tell me, each of the others, that they are thieves, robbers, arsonists, [all] qualities which all three attribute to the Italians' (quoted in Mombauer, 2003, p. 114).

A 'political consequence'?

EXERCISE

In a second extract from Diana Preston, 'The spoils of Peking', which is in the secondary sources on the course website, she describes the end of the rebellion, and the looting and violence that occurred. Read the text and summarise the behaviour of the victors in Peking.

Spend about 30–45 minutes on this exercise.

SPECIMEN ANSWER

The Chinese population was subjected to brutal reprisals; all of them were treated indiscriminately as Boxers and punished by the Europeans. The victors burnt and pillaged, and surpassed each other in looting the many treasures of the city. While Peking was ransacked by the military, the diplomats planned a victory parade in order to humiliate the Chinese even further. It is likely that such brutality was made possible by the racist notions about the Chinese that were in circulation at the time.

A number of general points can be drawn from this brief account of the Boxer Rebellion and the German response. First, although Wilhelm II's reactions were more extreme than most, he illustrates the way in which events in China were interpreted in terms of racial stereotypes, and prevailing views on how relations between Germans (and Europeans) and 'uncivilised' Asians should be conducted. Both Wilhelm and his General Waldersee constantly articulated racial prejudices and a belief in European superiority. The alleged 'cunning' of the Chinese was frequently mentioned by the monarch in his speeches to departing troops, and Waldersee echoed similar sentiments in his diary: 'Only if one behaves harshly and ruthlessly against them can one make progress with them', he wrote. Later, when negotiations with the Chinese court were still fraught, he noted: 'Because one cannot ever trust the Chinese completely, one still has to be careful here until the last moment' (quoted in Mombauer, 2003, pp. 115–16).

August 1900 (3 yrs after Bülow's speech)

Secondly, the events reveal some of the tensions surrounding Germany's relations with its European neighbours. The Kaiser's response to the Boxer Rebellion is best understood in the context of the wider sense of insecurity that prevailed among Germany's decision makers. In turn, the example demonstrates how German actions fostered hostility among the other great powers. The events in China unfolded against a volatile European background at a time when the two rival alliances that were to dominate European politics in the years leading up to the First World War were not yet fixed. For Germany, there was still everything to play for in terms of coming to an arrangement with Britain or France. France and Russia had become allies in 1894, but the cooperation between German and French troops in China suggested to some that there might now be scope for a future friendship. In the context of this uncertainty, the Kaiser was keen to prove to the world that Germany was a power to be reckoned with, and one whose friendship was worth coveting. Defeating the Boxer Rebellion was thus always about much more than simply dealing harshly with resistance to western encroachments. Wilhelm, and his future chancellor, Bülow, hoped to turn the European situation to Germany's advantage while also hoping that the other European powers, and particularly Russia, Britain and France, would fall out over China.

Consequence

Finally, and perhaps most importantly, Germany's actions during the Boxer Rebellion need to be seen in the context of German history at the end of the nineteenth century. The country's involvement in the Boxer Rebellion forms one of a string of foreign policy engagements, most of which did not show Germany in a positive light. German policy appeared, in the words of Klaus Hildebrand, to be 'directionless and aimlessly drifting', and it led to the alienation of the other powers. Among this seemingly directionless policy were

Germany's acquisition of Kiaochow, which is the subject of the French cartoon in the *Visual Sources*, Plate 24.2, and the purchase of some territories in the Pacific Ocean. Such sudden actions deepened the rift between Germany and the other great powers, and made it difficult to gauge the country's real intentions. It amounted, in Hildebrand's words, to a policy of 'wanting to be rewarded simply for being strong and present' (Hildebrand, 1989, p. 33; 1995, p. 193). In many ways, this also sums up adequately the reasons behind Germany's colonial expansion in the 1890s. By the time Bülow became chancellor in October 1900, Germany had become an increasingly unpredictable player who had managed to alienate its main great power rivals.

The Herero uprising

The causes of the rebellion

Other imperial wars involved Germany in a different way and without the help of allies. In the early twentieth century, the inhabitants of Germany's African colonies rebelled against their harsh treatment by German settlers and the colonial authorities. The following section looks at one of these rebellions.

After the First World War, when Germany lost, among others, its territories in Africa, the American President Woodrow Wilson came to a damning conclusion about the country's colonial endeavours. In his estimation, Germany

> had brought intolerable burdens and injustices on the helpless people of some of the colonies, which it annexed to itself; that its interest was rather their extermination than their development; that the desire was to possess their land for European purposes, and not to enjoy their confidence in order that mankind might be lifted in those places to the next higher level.
>
> (Quoted in Wirz, 1982, p. 388)

Of course it would be wrong to infer from this statement that all other colonial powers behaved impeccably towards the peoples in their colonies (you already know that terrible crimes against the local people were committed in the Congo); Wilson's comments need also to be placed in the context of the aftermath of the First World War for which Germany was blamed. However, as the following example of the Herero uprising of 1904 demonstrates, German colonial settlers and traders did pursue harsh policies towards the people of South-West Africa, and in the process of defeating the rebellion they all but exterminated the Herero and Nama peoples. The suppression of the resistance by the Herero also demonstrates how German (and other European) ideas about Africans and other non-European peoples contributed to the way the uprising was dealt with. The following section will explore the causes and course of the Herero uprising before looking at the controversy about the German response (see Figure 24.7).

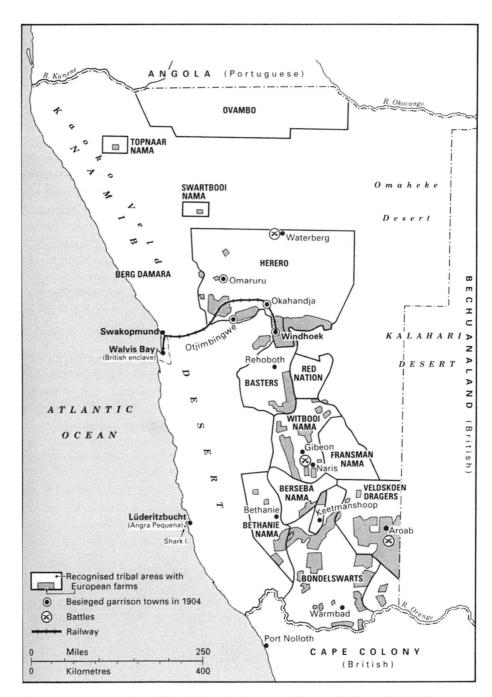

Figure 24.7   German South-West Africa: the Herero and Nama rebellions, 1904–5, from Thomas Pakenham, *The Scramble for Africa 1876–1912*, London, Weidenfeld and Nicolson, 1991, p. 603

German South-West Africa was first claimed by Germany in 1884 during Bismarck's brief foray into colonial expansion. A largely desert territory, with few inhabitants, the colony was of limited interest and value to Germany before the discovery of diamonds in 1908. However, it was seen as a possible colony of settlement and a trickle of immigrants meant that there were around 5,000 German settlers in the colony by 1904.

EXERCISE

You will find an account of the Herero uprising in Thomas Pakenham's 'The Kaiser's First War', which is in the secondary sources on the course website. Read the first section of this chapter, to the end of the paragraph beginning 'Far more would have died if the reservists had not …', on the causes and outbreak of the rebellion. Then jot down your answers to the following questions:

1   What does Pakenham suggest were the main causes of the uprising?

2   Why did the uprising break out in 1904 and not earlier?

3   Why was the uprising at first successful?

Spend about 45–60 minutes on this exercise.

SPECIMEN ANSWER

1   Two major causes for the uprising emerge from Pakenham's account. The first was economic. The best land in South-West Africa was the central plateau (see Figure 24.7) and even this was of limited agricultural value. The two main peoples that inhabited this area, the Herero and the Nama, were both semi-nomadic, relying on cattle grazing for their livelihoods. The poor quality of the land meant that they needed large areas for their cattle and, as the German population increased, there was competition for land. In many ways, this was a conflict about resources.

The tension between the settlers and the Herero was, however, made worse by the way that the settlers treated the local people. Pakenham contrasts the 'studied politeness' with which the German governor, Theodor von Leutwein, treated the leader of the Herero, Samuel Maherero, and the brutal way that other Germans treated his people.

2   When the Germans first arrived in South-West Africa, the Herero and the Nama were in conflict. Both sides hoped to profit from the new arrivals. Moreover, at first there were few Germans and their impact was minimal. The original treaties imposed few demands on the Herero and the Nama. It appears that there was a significant difference between the parties as to the meaning of the treaties. Only as the number of Germans rose did they threaten the Herero and the Nama. One might identify the completion of the railway from the coast to the capital, Windhoek, as evidence of the changing balance of forces.

The other event that changed the balance was the rinderpest epidemic of 1897. According to Pakenham, the Herero lost four-fifths of their cattle, so that by the early twentieth century they owned roughly as many as the Germans. The epidemic forced many Herero into paid labour for the Germans and into much closer contact.

3   The uprising was at first successful because it took place when most German troops were in the far south of the colony putting down another rebellion, the Bondelzwart uprising. The Germans also seem to have been taken by surprise. In any case, they had few troops in the colony. At the same time, the situation

could have been far worse for the Germans. You may have noted that the Herero failed in their attempt to persuade the Nama to join them. Although there were a number of uprisings against German rule between 1903 and 1907, there was little cooperation between the different peoples.

DISCUSSION

One might therefore identify two types of issue as leading to conflict. First, there were issues related to resources. At first the Germans made relatively little impact on the local population, but, over time, competition for land and water grew. The rinderpest epidemic had catastrophic results for the Herero. As a result of this disease, the Herero were forced to take paid work for the Germans and to buy food (often on credit) because they could no longer produce it for themselves. In order to profit from the Herero's plight, traders often charged inflated prices for their goods, so that many of the Herero ended up in debt (Bühler, 2003, pp. 103–4). Not only did this cause resentment among the Herero, but attempts by the German government to alleviate the problem only made matters worse. In an effort to regulate the indebtedness of the Herero to the German traders, the government passed the so-called *Kreditverordnung* (credit law), which intended to make instalment credit void after one year. However, the decision to give the traders only one year to collect their debts from the Herero before their claim expired resulted in unprecedented brutality against them (Bühler, 2003, p. 104). By 1904, the German settlers had the best grassland and had restricted the Herero's access to watering holes and the free movement of cattle. The Herero had largely been robbed of their cattle. When an official count took place in 1902, approximately 80,000 Herero owned 45,910 cattle, where previously they had owned hundreds of thousands, while a few hundred German settlers owned almost the same number, 44,490. The settlers had amassed a fortune of 20 million marks, 14 million of which was made up of cattle (Drechsler, 1984, p. 50). The building of the railway exacerbated the situation. It led straight through the Herero land, thus reducing precious grazing land even further, and they were expected to relinquish their land and access to water without any compensation (Drechsler, 1984, p. 52).

However, we should also note the second issue: the German treatment of the local people. The immediate cause for rebellion was often an individual act of cruelty or unfairness. A good example of this is the cause for the Bondelzwart uprising. In 1903, the German district chief, Lieutenant Jobst, had intervened in an internal dispute between the Bondelzwart captain, Abraham Christiaan, and a member of his tribe. This was one humiliation too far. Jobst and two other Germans were shot and the Germans reacted by proclaiming war and putting a cash prize on the culprits (Zimmerer, 2001, p. 31).

Discrimination by the German authorities was legalised. White offenders who had committed a crime against Hereros often went unpunished, even for serious offences such as murder and rape, while, for example, the flogging of African servants not only went unpunished, but was actually permitted. In a lawsuit, it was the general rule that the testimony of seven Africans was needed to count as much as that of one white man (Bühler, 2003, pp. 109ff). An infamous example of the lawlessness to which the Herero were exposed was the case of Prince Prosper von Arenberg. He had already been convicted for mistreating a subordinate in Germany and was sent to German South-West Africa. Here he claimed to have unearthed a smugglers' group and so had the Herero Willi Cain arrested on 24 September 1899. Cain denied the charge of intending to flee with his men and cattle over the border. He was beaten and threatened, and later taken to his village where his father and two of his men were also arrested. After a drunken night, Arenberg allowed Cain to flee and then had him shot, attempting to finish the job himself with a shot to Cain's head. Cain was still not dead, and Arenberg had him bayoneted twice and committed other acts of cruelty against him. As punishment for this horrible crime, Arenberg was initially sentenced to 10 months in prison. After protests in Germany, particularly from the Social Democrat press, he was re-tried and received a death sentence in September 1900; however, following a personal intervention from the Kaiser, that sentence was reduced to 15 years imprisonment. After the Herero uprising, Arenberg was again re-tried and this time let off, on account of insanity at the time of the crime (Drechsler, 1984, pp. 53–4). Such examples demonstrate the discrimination against the Herero, and do much to explain their resentment and eventual uprising against their oppressors.

EXERCISE

When we looked at the extract from Else Sonnenberg's narrative, we already noted how European ideas about Africa were formed. Anthology Document 6.16, 'German settlers and the Herero uprising, 1904', extract (b) 'Relations between the German settlers and the Herero', is the second extract from her account. Read the second paragraph of this extract, starting with the second sentence beginning 'Every now and then, some resentment …' (you are, of course, welcome to read the whole extract!).

Spend just a few minutes on this activity.

DISCUSSION

The passage brings out very well how the attitudes of the Germans towards the Herero people raised tensions. I hope you also noted, however, that Sonnenberg suggests that there were differences of opinion among the German settlers and that the story of the trader she recounts does not reflect well on the Germans. As we noted in Unit 21, it is at times helpful to differentiate between underlying and widely held beliefs about race, which were often unspoken, and the conclusions and behaviour based on them, where less consensus may have existed.

The course of the Herero uprising

At first, the Herero, under the leadership of Maherero, were successful. With few German troops in central South-West Africa, they were able to attack and destroy many of the isolated farms, although they had less success against the garrison towns. As Pakenham notes, many German male settlers and traders were killed and some were tortured or their bodies mutilated. These events were seized upon in German accounts of the uprising. See, for instance, the two illustrations (Figures 24.8 and 24.9) from popular contemporary accounts, which show the Herero as cunning and brutal.

Contemporary observers interpreted events as part of a racial struggle for supremacy. Some blamed the uprising on the 'bloodlust' of the Herero, a feature of some of the propaganda of the period (see Figure 24.9). However, according to Horst Drechsler, this representation is 'particularly absurd, because the Hereros spared English, Boers and missionaries as well as the

Figure 24.8 'The revenge of the Herero', from Steffen Jonk, *Okowi: ein Hererospion? Eine Geschichte aus dem südwestafrikanischen Kriege,* Berlin, 1910, reprinted in Zimmerer and Zeller, 2003, p. 91

Figure 24.9   Propaganda from a contemporary colonial book, intended to help justify the expensive and increasingly unpopular war to a German audience, from Friedrich Frhr. v. Dincklage-Campe, *Deutsche Reiter in Südwest: Selbsterlebniße aus den Kämpfen in Deutsch-Südwestafrika,* Berlin, 1910, reprinted in Zimmerer and Zeller, 2003, p. 157

women and children of the German settlers' (Drechsler, 1984, p. 55). You may have noted this point when reading Pakenham.

EXERCISE

Else Sonnenberg's account describes the Herero uprising vividly. Read Anthology Document 6.16, 'German settlers and the Herero uprising, 1904', extract (c) 'Else Sonnenberg's account of the attack of the Herero on her family'. How do the events appear to this witness? Does this account lend credence to Drechsler's interpretation?

Spend about 15–30 minutes on this exercise.

SPECIMEN ANSWER

Clearly, these were shocking events. Only shortly after they occurred, the author is attempting to give an impression of the dramatic goings-on which led to the death of her husband. It is perhaps hardly surprising that she has no understanding of (or does not seek to understand) the causes for this brutal attack. She likens the attackers to animals, and questions whether the people who were committing these atrocities against her and her family could really be human. The Herero certainly appear very bloodthirsty in this account. However, in confirmation of Drechsler's interpretation, it is also true that the women and the baby were spared and did not suffer the fate of the German male settlers.

DISCUSSION

In her subsequent account, Else Sonnenberg describes how she manages to survive by living with the missionary's family, and that no harm is done to her and her baby son (although they continue to live in fear of their lives until they are rescued by the arrival of German troops). By the end of January, the situation had changed and the German troops had the upper hand. Leutwein ended the war with the Bondelzwart in order to avoid a two-front war, and by mid-February he was back in Windhoek and had taken control of the situation.

EXERCISE

Now continue with your reading of Pakenham's account, 'The Kaiser's First War', in the secondary sources on the course website. Read the second section, which begins 'Perhaps it was inevitable that in Berlin ...' and ends with the paragraph that begins 'The battle of Waterberg on 11–12 August was predictably indecisive'. In this section, Pakenham describes the reaction of the Berlin government to the news of the uprising, and the difference in approach between Leutwein and the new military leader sent out by Berlin, General Lothar von Trotha, on the ground. How did his policy differ from that of Leutwein?

Spend about 20 minutes on this exercise.

SPECIMEN ANSWER

It would be wrong to imagine that Leutwein was a soft ruler. In the earlier section from Pakenham we read his brutal assessment that 'colonization is always inhumane'. However, in the summer of 1904, once the Germans had the upper hand, he advocated negotiation. On economic grounds, if none other, he was concerned that the colony would be ruined by too destructive a war. However, Trotha was determined to carry out his orders from Berlin and force the Herero into an unconditional surrender. By August 1904, the Herero had been cornered on the Waterberg plateau and, after a final battle, they were forced into the Omaheke desert.

EXERCISE

Now read the final section from Pakenham, from where you left off in the previous exercise to the end and summarise the response in Berlin to von Trotha's strategy.

Spend about 20 minutes on this exercise.

SPECIMEN ANSWER

As Pakenham notes, when the Herero uprising first broke out, there was little opposition in Germany to the government's response. However, as news of German atrocities got back to Germany, protests grew. More significantly, concerns emerged in the army and the political elite. The chief of the general staff, Alfred von Schlieffen, began to have doubts about Trotha's ability to carry out his plans (considering his intentions 'commendable' but him 'powerless to carry them out'). Instead, Schlieffen advocated trying to induce the Herero to surrender. After some debate with the Kaiser, Chancellor Bülow managed to persuade him to give permission to cable Trotha to show mercy to the Herero, and eventually Trotha was ordered to cancel the 'extermination order' (*Vernichtungsbefehl*). However, Trotha initially refused to cooperate.

The results of the war against the Herero

As Pakenham makes clear, the war had a disastrous effect on the Herero people. Many died in the Omahake desert, and those who survived were in a critical condition. Plate 24.3 in the *Visual Sources* is a photo taken of some of the survivors. Nor did their suffering end there. Although the conduct of the war did lead to protests (Figure 24.10 shows a cartoon that appeared in a German satirical paper at the time), this did not stop the German government implementing grave measures against the Herero following the war. In 1905, all the Herero's possessions were expropriated (Wilhelm II signed the law to this effect on 26 December 1905, despite protests from the *Reichstag* members Erzberger and Bebel), and all the land and cattle were taken. The same happened to the tribe of the Nama after their defeat in 1907 (Bley, 1968, pp. 208ff). The so-called *Eingeborenenverordnung* (natives' law) of 1906/07 ruled that the lands of all the people who had rebelled were to be taken from them, that their tribal organisations were to be broken up, and that they were to be prohibited from keeping cattle. One of the intentions behind these measures was to destroy the community within the tribe. To achieve this it was, for example, ruled that no more than ten families or single workers were allowed to live in any one place. In order to clamp down on the Herero's nomadic lifestyle, all Africans over 8 years of age were required to wear an identifying metal tag around their necks, and they needed a special passport if they wanted to leave the district. Africans who were not in paid employment were treated as vagrants, thus making the traditional nomadic way of life even more impossible (Bley, 1968, pp. 211–12).

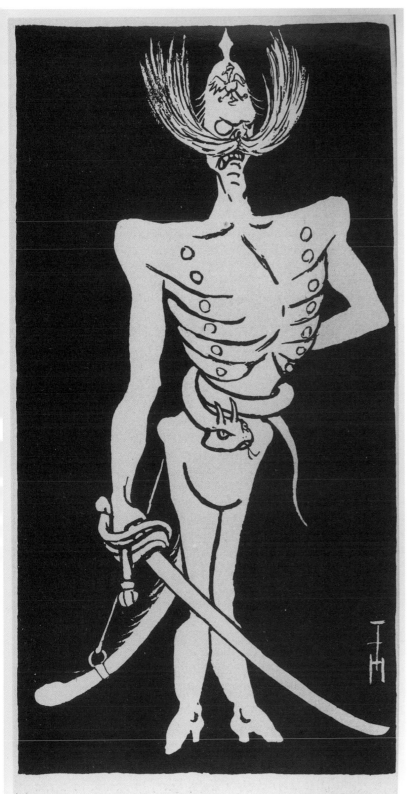

Wie die Neger in unsern Kolonien sich den Teufel vorstellen.

Figure 24.10 Thomas Theodor Heine, 'How the negroes in our colonies picture the devil', cartoon in *Simplicissimus*, no. 6, 1904. Abteilung Historische Drucke, Staatsbibliothek zu Berlin - Preußischer Kulturbesitz. Photo: BPK / Carola Seifert

The debate on genocide

As a result of the Herero uprising and the German response, 80 per cent of the Herero people were killed. Nama losses in the subsequent rebellion, which took much longer to defeat, were close to 50 per cent (Bühler, 2003, pp. 10–11). Many died in the fighting or from hunger or thirst, but many also died in prison or forced labour camps.

Historians have debated whether the German treatment of the Herero amounts to genocide. Before we look at this in detail, do the following exercise.

EXERCISE

Read the following quotation from the official history of the war against the Herero, which was published by the German General Staff in 1907.

> No effort, no privations were spared in order to rob the enemy of the last remnant of his power to resist; like game that has been chased to near-death he was chased from watering-hole to watering-hole until finally, weak-willed, he became a victim of his own country. The arid Omaheke [desert] was to finish what German weapons had begun: the extermination of the Herero people.
>
> (cited in Bühler, 2003, p. 136)

What do you notice about the language used in this official history to describe the Herero people and the German actions?

Spend about 5–10 minutes on this exercise.

SPECIMEN ANSWER

The official historian clearly saw no need to present the German actions in a good light. No accusation of genocide had yet been made, and there was no need to whitewash Germany's policy in South-West Africa. The Herero are likened to animals. They had been chased by the German soldiers 'like game' into ever more arid terrain. But the cause of the many deaths that the Herero suffered was, in this interpretation, nature itself, rather than the German military. The Herero were victims 'of their own country'. In this official military version of events, the Herero are completely de-humanised. Their suffering in the Omaheke desert is downplayed and their death almost incidental to the military campaign that had preceded it.

Did Germany's policy against the Herero amount to genocide? The *Oxford English Dictionary* defines genocide as: 'the *deliberate* killing of a very large number of people from a particular ethnic group or nation' (my emphasis). If intention is important, then the 'extermination order', which Pakenham quotes and which he suggests had 'few parallels in modern European history' is clearly important. You may find it useful to look at Trotha's order again.

 If intentions are crucial, Trotha's order seems to be clear evidence that the treatment of the Herero did indeed amount to genocide. In terms of German history, such a claim is, of course, explosive, but it also needs to be seen in an African context. Trotha's order has been used to make a distinction between events in the Congo and in South-West Africa: while far more died in the Congo, it was, for Hochschild, 'not, strictly speaking, a genocide. The Congo state was not deliberately trying to eliminate one particular ethnic group'. On the other hand, events in South-West Africa were 'genocide, pure and simple, starkly announced in advance' (Hochschild, 2002, pp. 225, 281).

DVD exercise

Now turn to DVD 3. In the final section, we have provided you with a 10-minute excerpt from a BBC documentary on the German war against the Herero and Nama tribes, entitled *Namibia: Genocide and the Second Reich.* You pick up the story at the point when General von Trotha is appointed. As you watch the film, do not just look for information about events (although this is one purpose of the DVD); you should also ask yourself how the question of genocide is addressed in the film. What importance is attached to the 'extermination order'? How does it fit into German policy? Is any evidence presented which might undermine the view that a deliberate policy of genocide was pursued?

You may want to watch the clip twice, hence the longer time estimate for this exercise. You will find further information about the DVD in the *Media Guide*.

Spend about 20–30 minutes on this exercise.

SPECIMEN ANSWER

The DVD starts with von Trotha's appointment and his journey to German South-West Africa. It emphasises how this changed the situation: Trotha was not prepared to negotiate with the Herero and was determined to win an overwhelming military victory – the rules of the game had changed. The 'extermination order' is given due significance and is presented as following logically from this new policy. The DVD does not suggest that there might be any doubt that genocide occurred.

Although not a great deal is made of it, the DVD does present some evidence that raises questions about who was responsible for policy. It explains that the 'extermination order' was greeted with shock in Berlin and that there were big protests: Trotha's actions were described by some opposition figures as a national scandal.

DISCUSSION

As presented in the DVD, the genocide in South-West Africa is not a subject of debate. I think this is a good example of what is sometimes amiss with TV history. While the programme makers have obviously done a great job at telling the story (and, despite the fact that there is no moving image of the events, have still managed to use the TV format to excellent effect!), they have a particular point of view that they want to bring across, and little if any time for contradictory positions.

For historians, things are not quite so straightforward: there has indeed been fierce debate on this topic. One part of the debate concerns the meaning of the 'extermination order'. What led Trotha to issue it? What exactly did it mean? To explore this debate, we will consider two articles on the subject. You will find links to both articles on the course website.

EXERCISE

The first article, by Tilman Dedering, is entitled 'The German Herero war of 1904: revisionism of genocide or imaginary historiography'. In it, he reviews (and indeed attacks) the work of another historian, Brigitte Lau. Although you are welcome to read the whole article, for this exercise you only need to read from the beginning to the foot of p. 84 '... and faced a horrible fate'.

Read this section and then answer the following questions:

1   How does Dedering summarise Brigitte Lau's critique of Horst Drechsler's view of the Herero uprising?

2   What is the importance of the 'extermination order' to Lau? What does Dedering make of this criticism?

Spend about 20–30 minutes on this exercise.

SPECIMEN ANSWER

1   According to Dedering, Lau accuses Drechsler of not knowing anything about Namibia and denies his claim that the Herero were the victims of genocide. Her two main criticisms of Drechsler concern his concept of genocide and the documentary evidence he used. She accuses him of being Eurocentric in portraying Africans as helpless victims, and alleges that his view is influenced by his knowledge of later events, namely the Holocaust, leading him to identify continuities that can only be seen with hindsight.

2   Lau emphasises that the order was issued two months after the key battle of the war and that it should be seen as 'psychological warfare' (p. 82). Dedering does not accept this. He argues that the order was not related to the battle on the Waterberg, but was conceived in racist terms as an attempt to destroy the Herero people. Trotha's orders are 'irrefutable evidence of the military leadership's intentions' and Drechsler's use of them as part of his argument for genocide seems justified (p. 83).

Although Dedering argues against 'linear continuity between the extermination of the Herero and the Holocaust forty years later' (p. 83), he clearly agrees with Drechsler and others that the actions against the Herero amounted to genocide, rejecting the claims of revisionists. If Lau downplays the importance of the order, for Dedering it is a key text: clear evidence of the policy of the military leadership.

EXERCISE

The second link is to a recent article by Isabel Hull, 'The military campaign in German Southwest Africa, 1904–1907'. Again you do not need to read the whole article. Start your reading on p. 40 at 'For the Germans...' and read through to '... World War I' on p. 42. Then answer the following questions.

1   Does Hull think the war against the Herero was a genocide?

2   How does her analysis of the 'extermination order' differ from that of Dedering?

3   What, for Hull, was the cause of genocide?

Spend about 15 minutes on this exercise.

SPECIMEN ANSWER

1 Yes, she is quite clear. On p. 40 she describes the war 'as the first genocide of the twentieth century'.

2 Like Lau, Hull highlights the fact that the order came after most Herero had died. Her explanation for this is different, however, from that of Lau or of Dedering. Whereas Dedering sees events as the result of German planning, Hull emphasises mistakes. The order came out of failure and was partly meant to provide a retrospective justification 'for the genocide that had already occurred' (p. 41).

3 For Hull, 'genocide developed out of standard military practices and assumptions' (p. 41). She emphasises that European military tactics transferred to Africa resulted in mass deaths. She suggests that this conclusion has alarming implications: 'in some ways, it is comforting to think that racist beliefs are primarily responsible for genocide, for that enables us to distance ourselves from the perpetrators and to imagine that only ideological fanatics could produce this kind of mass death' (p. 42).

DISCUSSION

Hull's analysis suggests another way of looking at events in South-West Africa and the Congo, and indeed in other African colonies. In discussing these events, we should perhaps focus less on intentions and more on practice. The agents of European empires may not have set out to exterminate peoples in Africa, but when they used their greater power the results were often mass deaths. This, however, did not lead to a reassessment. Instead, imperialists sought justifications that explained events, explanations which were often based on race: as Hull argues, 'racism is often the product rather than the cause of colonialism and its horrors' (p. 42).

As you will have seen in this brief discussion of a complex and emotive issue, unpacking even seemingly straightforward texts can reveal layers of complexity. Part of such historical debates is understanding what happened and why it did – by placing the 'extermination order' in a slightly different context, Hull provides a new analysis of events that adds to a wider understanding of how genocides occur. It seems, however, unlikely that she will have the last word on the subject – debates about European atrocities in Africa during the colonial period are likely to continue. You may recall from DVD 3 section 2 the comments by Guido Gryseels, the director of the Africa Museum in Brussels, about how difficult it was for the museum to put on the 2005 exhibition 'Memory of Congo'. In other European countries, too, there is often a reluctance to confront the history of the colonial period and considerable debate about how such events should be remembered.

CONCLUSIONS TO BLOCK 6

Although this block has focused on a briefer timespan than the previous five, it has covered a wide range of topics, including both broad debates, such as the causes of the 'new imperialism' of the late nineteenth century, and detailed case studies. Looking at the imperialism of three European countries has made it possible to identify differences and similarities, for instance, in attitudes to expansion. In terms of the course themes, the block has considered imperial trade and economic expectations (producers and consumers); how expansion was linked to certain ideas of the state and national prestige (state formation); and the interplay between ideas about non-European peoples and imperial policies (beliefs and ideologies). The debate about the causes of imperialism has highlighted economic, political and strategic, and cultural factors. What has been most striking, perhaps, is how difficult it is to separate the three. Thus, for instance, whereas it is hard to demonstrate an economic cause for many of the late nineteenth-century imperial acquisitions in Africa, expectations of gain, themselves rooted in beliefs about Africa and about imperialism, were clearly a factor. Moreover, once colonial rule had been established, imperial powers were able to use their power to reshape economies to their advantage, or at least to the advantage of metropolitan groups or individuals.

consequences ?

Two final points: throughout the block, the emphasis has been on imperialism and Europe. It need hardly be said that imperialism also had a dramatic impact on other continents, and this we have barely touched on (even in the discussion of resistance to imperialism in China and South-West Africa, the focus was kept on German responses to resistance). Broadening the units to include the history of imperialism from an African or Asian perspective would have added greatly to the complexity of the material. But the focus on Europe is not merely for reasons of space: in recent years historians have emphasised the extent to which empire and imperialism came to suffuse all aspects of metropolitan life. How deep or lasting was the impact is a subject of debate, as you learnt in Unit 21 where you read two rather different views from Said and Marshall.

Secondly, and following on from the above, we have tried to show the importance of debates between historians in developing our knowledge and understanding of the past. In several places, the fact that historians are embedded in a culture has been emphasised: as relations between Europe and its former colonies have changed, so too have the interests and attitudes of historians. As we write, globalisation is the issue of the day and historians are reviewing history in terms of 'imperial globalisation'. It is easy to be cynical and see this in terms of fads, and there is of course some truth in this. But historians also need to provide evidence to back their cases, and use or reuse the material legacy of the past as new questions arise in the present. New documents may be found or old ones reinterpreted, but we cannot simply set them aside. So too with the arguments of historians who have preceded us: we may disagree, but it would be foolish to ignore them. Thus the debate between historians is not simply a clash of views, but should be a constant pushing out of frontiers as we build on the learning of the past.

REFERENCES

Berghahn, V. (1994) *Imperial Germany, 1871–1918. Economy, Society, Culture and Politics*, Providence/Oxford, Berghahn Books.

Bley, H. (1968) *Kolonialherrschaft und Sozialstruktur in Deutsch-Südwestafrika, 1894–1914*, Hamburg, Leibniz Verlag.

Bruch, R. vom and Hofmeister, B. (eds) (2000) *Deutsche Geschichte in Quellen und Darstellung*, vol. 8, *Kaiserreich und Erster Weltkrieg 1871–1918*, Stuttgart, Reclam.

Bühler, A.H. (2003) *Der Namaaufstand gegen die deutsche Kolonialherrschaft in Namibia von 1904–1913*, Frankfurt/London, IKO Verlag für Interkulturelle Kommunikation.

Bülow, B. Fürst von (1930) *Denkwürdigkeiten*, Berlin, Ullstein.

Dedering, T. (1993) 'The German Herero war of 1904: revisionism of genocide or imaginary historiography', *Journal of Southern African Studies*, vol. 19, pp. 80–8.

Drechsler, H. (1984) *Aufstände in Südwest-Afrika*, Berlin, Dietz Verlag.

Felber, R. and Rostek H (1987) *Der "Hunnenkrieg" Kaiser Wilhelms II. Imperialistische Intervention in China, 1900/01*, East Berlin, Illustrierte Historische Hefte 45.

Geiss, I. (1976) *German Foreign Policy 1871–1914*, London, Routledge & Keegan Paul.

Heyden, U. van der and Zeller, J. (2002) *Kolonialmetropole Berlin. Eine Spurensuche*, Berlin, Berlin Edition.

Hildebrand, K. (1989) *Deutsche Aussenpolitik 1871–1918. Enzyklopädie Deutscher Geschichte*, vol. 2, Munich, Oldenbourg.

Hildebrand, K. (1995) *Das vergangene Reich*, Stuttgart, Deutsche Verlagsanstalt.

Hochschild, A. (2002 [1998]) *King Leopold's Ghost. A Story of Greed, Terror and Heroism in Colonial Africa*, Pan Macmillan, London.

Hull, I.V. (2005) 'The military campaign in German Southwest Africa, 1904–1907', *Bulletin of the German Historical Institute*, vol. 37, pp. 39–44.

Lepsius, J., Mendelsohn-Bartholdy, A. and Thimme, F. (eds) (1922–1927) *Die Grosse Politik der europäischen Kabinette*, Berlin, Deutsche Verlagsgesellschaft.

Mohs, H. (1929) *General-Feldmarschall Alfred Graf von Waldersee in seinem militärischen Wirken*, Berlin, Einsenschmidt.

Mombauer, A. (2003) 'Wilhelm, Waldersee and the Boxer Rebellion' in Mombauer, A. and Deist, W. (eds) *The Kaiser. New Research on Wilhelm II's Role in Imperial Germany*, Cambridge, Cambridge University Press.

Nipperdey, T. (1994) *Deutsche Geschichte,* vol. 2. *1866–1918*, Munich, Beck.

Pakenham, T. (1991) *The Scramble for Africa 1876–1912*, London, Weidenfeld & Nicolson.

Penzler, J. (ed.) (1904) *Die Reden Kaiser Wilhelms II in den Jahren 1896 bis 1900*, 2. Teil, Leipzig, Philipp Reclam.

Röhl, J.C. R. (2001) *Wilhelm II. Der Aufbau der Persönlichen Monarchie*, Munich, C.H. Beck.

Sonnenberg, E. (1905) *Wie es damals am Waterberg zuging. Ein Beitrag zur Geschichte des Hereroaufstandes*, Berlin, Wilhelm Süsserott Verlagsbuchhandlung.

Wirz, A. (1982) 'The German colonies in Africa' in Albertini, R. von (ed.) *European Colonial Rule 1880–1940. The Impact of the West on India, Southeast Asia, and Africa* (trans. J.G. Williamson), Oxford, Clio Press.

Young, L.K. (1970) *British Policy in China, 1895–1902*, Oxford, Clarendon Press.

Zimmerer, J. (2001) *Deutsche Herrschaft über Afrikaner. Staatlicher Machtanspruch und Wirklichkeit im kolonialen Namibia*, Münster, LIT Verlag.

Zimmerer, J. and Zeller, J. (eds) (2003) *Völkermord in Deutsch-Südwestafrika. Der Kolonialkrieg (1904–1908) in Namibia und seine Folgen*, Berlin, Ch. Links Verlag.

FURTHER READING

Ascherson, N. (1999 [1963]) *The King Incorporated. Leopold the Second and the Congo*, London, Granta.

Bayly, C.A. (2004) *The Birth of the Modern World 1780–1914*, Oxford, Blackwell.

Berghahn, V. (1994) *Imperial Germany, 1871–1918. Economy, Society, Culture and Politics*, Providence/Oxford, Berghahn Books.

Cain, P.J. and Hopkins, A.G. (1993) *British Imperialism. Innovation and Expansion, 1688–1914*, London, Longman.

Cain, P.J. and Hopkins, A.G. (1993) *British Imperialism. Crisis and Deconstruction, 1914–1990*, London, Longman.

Gordon, E. (1991) *Women and the Labour Movement in Scotland, 1850–1914*, Oxford, Clarendon Press.

Hochschild, A. (2002) *King Leopold's Ghost. A Story of Greed, Terror and Heroism in Colonial Africa*, London, Pan.

Kennedy, D. (2002) *Britain and Empire 1880-1945*, Harlow, Longman.

Marshall, P.J. (ed.) (1996) *The Cambridge Illustrated History of the British Empire*, Cambridge, Cambridge University Press.

Miskell, L., Whatley, C.A. and Harris, B. (eds) (2000) *Victorian Dundee. Images and Realities*, East Linton, Tuckwell.

Nelson, S. (1994) *Colonialism in the Congo Basin, 1880–1940*, Athens, Ohio, Ohio University Center for International Studies.

Thompson, A. (2005) *The Empire Strikes Back? The Impact of Imperialism on Britain from the Mid-nineteenth Century*, Harlow, Pearson Longman.

Walker, W. (1979) *Juteopolis: Dundee and its Textile Workers, 1885–1923*, Edinburgh, Scottish Academic Press.

Wesseling, H.L. (2004) *The European Colonial Empires, 1815–1919*, Harlow, Pearson Longman.

GLOSSARY

Afrikaner
An Afrikaans-speaking white person in South Africa. Afrikaans is a South African language derived from Dutch. Term often used interchangeably with **Boer** (see below).

annex
To take territory without approval or formal permission.

anthropology
The comparative study of humankind. Despite its claims to scientific status in the nineteenth century, anthropological studies tended to attach value to the differences observed in societies, with some western societies deemed to be more civilised and advanced than other, non-western societies.

Association Internationale du Congo (AIC)
International Association of the Congo. The name of the organisation set up by Leopold II in the early 1880s to lobby for a Congo trading zone. Although called an international association, the organisation was largely controlled by Leopold II. Following successful diplomatic lobbying at the Berlin Conference, the zone was recognised as the Congo Free State.

balance sheet
A statement of the wealth of a business on a given date, usually the last date of the financial year. A balance sheet will show liabilities on one side and assets on the other. Both columns will show the same total, with the shareholders' capital (the equity) shown in the liability column.

barriers to entry
Economic or technical factors that prevent or make it difficult for firms to enter a market and compete with existing suppliers.

Boers
Non-African population of South Africa descended from Dutch and Huguenot (French protestant) settlers in the late seventeenth century. The Boers were typically farmers. The word is derived from the Dutch for farmer and was widely used by English-speaking South Africans. See also **Afrikaner** above.

colonisation
The process of establishing control and influence over a people or country.

competitive advantage
The specific factors that might give one competitor an advantage in a particular business. The term is often used to describe factors that it is difficult to challenge, such as natural resources or geographical location.

concessionary company
A company that is allotted a grant of land and other property from a government in exchange for rent or other commitments. The system was used in some African colonies, including the Congo, to develop exports. In the Congo Free State, concessionary companies, such as ABIR, were granted large tracts for exploitation, on 30-year leases. The government of the Free State shared in the profits.

Congo Free State

The État indépendant du Congo was the name of the central African state established by Leopold II in 1885. The state was recognised as an independent state and survived until it was taken over by Belgium in 1908.

decolonisation

The withdrawal of a colonial power from a colony, usually resulting in the latter's independence.

depreciation

The reduction in value of an asset through wear and tear. A company should make an allowance for the depreciation of its assets before the calculation of profits. For a manufacturing company, the main depreciation is likely to occur to buildings and machinery. There are different methods for calculating depreciation, but, in the late nineteenth century, the most usual method was to take the previous year's valuation, add the cost of any investment, and subtract a percentage (this is a form of historic-cost depreciation).

dividends

See **shares and dividends**.

empire

Group of states or countries dominated by one government. An empire can be establishment through formal systems of rule or informally constituted through trade agreements and/or cultural influence.

ethnography

The study of people through close observation of their culture and characteristics. In the nineteenth century, ethnography was sometimes used to classify humankind along racial lines.

free trade

An economic policy that advocates removing or reducing as far as possible government restrictions on trade, such as tariffs or other legal barriers to commerce. From the 1840s into the 1920s, Britain claimed to follow a free-trade policy and did abolish or reduce most tariffs.

genocide

The deliberate killing of a very large number of people from a particular ethnic group or nation.

gentlemanly capitalism

A phrase used by P. J. Cain and A. G. Hopkins to describe the form of capitalism that they claim dominated British policy from the eighteenth century to the twentieth century. A 'gentlemanly capitalist' elite was formed by the alliance and later merger of the landed aristocracy and the financial interests associated with the City of London.

gold standard

A currency system in which the value of money is tied to a fixed amount of gold held in reserves by a country. Under the gold standard, paper money should be convertible back to gold at any time. The gold standard became popular in the late nineteenth century as a way of limiting inflation by restricting the amount of paper money that could be produced. By the 1880s, a number of nations, including Britain, Germany, France and Belgium, used the gold standard.

great powers

A term much used in the nineteenth century to describe the most powerful countries in Europe. Since, for much of the nineteenth century, there existed a balance of power in Europe in which no 'super-power' dominated, alliances and conferences between the great powers were of great importance.

hegemony

The dominance of one group over another. The term is most closely associated with Antonio Gramsci (1891–1937). His theory of hegemony argued that dominance was orchestrated by intellectuals who were able to establish the pre-eminence of their ideas as natural, normal, and therefore not open to challenge.

imperialism

The process of extending power and influence over another country by force, persuasion or agreement.

imperial preference

A trade policy proposed in the 1900s that aimed to encourage trade within the British empire. One part of this was to impose a tariff on goods from outside the empire.

informal empire

A term used by historians of empire to describe a sphere of influence beyond the frontiers of the formal empire, in which British power was paramount. Because the influence was informal, it is hard to draw a precise boundary to this sphere of influence.

limited liability

The restriction of an owner's liabilities, and therefore potential losses, in a business to the amount of capital that he has invested in it. The 1856 Act allowed British companies to register as limited liability companies.

Maxim gun

The first self-powered machine gun invented by Sir Hiram Maxim in 1883. The gun was more powerful and destructive than other machine guns, such as the Gatling gun. The Maxim gun was used to brutal effect in the British and other imperial wars in Africa in the late nineteenth century.

mercantilism

A government policy that seeks to maximise national wealth, chiefly by restricting imports and encouraging exports.

metropole, metropolis

In discussions of empires, the term metropole or metropolis is used to describe the centre of an empire, as opposed to the 'periphery' – the colonies.

new journalism

Term used to refer to the expansion in production of cheap daily newspapers in the late nineteenth century. These papers, such as the *Daily Mail*, were aimed at a new audience of lower-middle-class and upper-working-class readers. The journalism was more sensationalist in tone than the established newspapers such as *The Times* and often contained images alongside stories.

Occident

West. Frequently used to mean Europe or, perhaps Europe and North America, when a stark and perhaps unbridgeable contrast is being drawn between European and Asian civilisations.

Orient

East. The opposite pole to the **Occident** (see above). Usually meaning China and the Far East, but often also the very different societies of India and South Asia and sometimes even the Middle East.

Orientalism

Traditionally refers to the study of eastern cultures and societies. More recently the term has been associated with the work of Edward Said and used to refer to the way political and intellectual culture constructs ideas about the west and non-west in relation to each other.

partnership

In business terms, an unincorporated business in which the partners share fully in the risks and profits of the business. Partners are fully liable for the debts of the company.

patriotism

Support for one's country. The term is often used to refer to romantic forms of popular nationalism. In history, forms of patriotism have drawn on ideas of the nation to challenge and support the government of the day.

protectorate

A state or territory placed or taken under the protection of a stronger power. Protectorates were often declared by colonial powers over territories where they did not wish to create extensive new systems of government. Existing authorities were allowed to continue, but were now subordinated to the colonial authorities. In practice, of course, colonial rule meant that power relations were irrevocably changed.

Reichstag

The German parliament

shares and dividends

Shares are the equal portions in the capital of a limited liability company; they entitle the owners to share in the profits of a company. Dividends are the amount of the profits that the directors decide to distribute per share at regular intervals (usually annually). A company may have different classes of shares, of which the most usual are preference and ordinary shares. Preference shares are due a fixed dividend each year and must be paid first. The dividends on ordinary shares fluctuate from year to year, depending on how much of the profits the directors decide is available for distribution. The risks of ordinary shares are greater, but the rewards are potentially higher.

social Darwinism

The appropriation of Charles Darwin's (1809–1882) theories of evolution and Herbert Spencer's (1820–1903) concept of the 'survival of the fittest' to define, classify and order the populations of different societies. Darwin's theory of the evolution of the species was applied to the development of human races to identify superior and inferior races and used to justify imperial expansion and white domination. The concept of 'survival of the fittest' became popular in the late nineteenth century to explain and validate the competition of social groups for pre-eminence.

social imperialism

A term used by historians to describe the pursuit of an expansionary imperialist policy for internal reasons; for instance, because it was hoped that successful overseas conquests would reduce social tensions.

subaltern

The term is used in the history of empire to refer to the powerless, the dominated and the oppressed, whose voice has been marginalised by those in power.

surplus capital

Money left over beyond what is wanted or needed. The term is used by theorists of empire to describe excess profits made in a capitalist system through the payment of unfairly low wages and the failure to reinvest in industry and manufacture. Surplus capital, therefore, is socially valueless surplus wealth.

tariffs and tariff wars

Custom duties imposed on imports. A tariff war is when two or more states impose high tariffs in retaliation for perceived unfair tariffs imposed by the other side.

tariff reform

A trade policy advocated in Britain in the early twentieth century which proposed that Britain should introduce tariffs against those countries that imposed tariffs on British goods. Tariff reform was often linked to **imperial preference** (see above).

valuation rolls

Lists of properties compiled annually in Scotland for the purpose of local taxation. The lists included all property and its rentable value. The English equivalent was named rate-books.

Weltpolitik

Literally, 'world policy'. The name given to Germany's foreign policy under Kaiser Wilhelm II, which combined a desire to increase Germany's prestige in the world, with obtaining tangible benefits such as colonies.

Bernard Waites

Now that you have nearly completed A200 it is time to reflect upon the course and pull together its main themes. This conclusion will help you do that by comparing two political entities which figure prominently near the beginning and near the end of A200: Burgundy and Belgium. This is an apt comparison because it allows us to contrast medieval and modern *state formation* in one small, but strategically crucial part of Europe, namely the Low Countries. In making this contrast, we will note how changes in the Low Countries' political geography between the late fifteenth and mid nineteenth century articulated with religious *beliefs* and political *ideologies*. (I will explain what I mean by 'articulated with' later.) We will also observe how the creation of the Belgian nation state followed closely on the industrialisation of the Belgian economy after 1815. There was no sudden transition to urban society: the southern Netherlands have been the most urbanised region north of the Alps since the Middle Ages. But new industrial towns and villages mushroomed on or near the Belgian coalfield, and production processes were transformed in iron and steel, textiles and glass-making. With the emergence of modern industry came a new class of *producers* (industrial wage earners) and new *consumer* markets. Whether there was a causal relationship between industrialisation and national state formation in this instance is debatable. But the Belgian case provides an interesting test for the theories of modern nationalism discussed by Paul Lawrence in Unit 19.

We will be making bold comparisons across time so to help orient you chronologically here are some key dates:

Burgundy, the Burgundian Netherlands and the Dutch revolt	Modern Belgium
1363: Philip the Bold invested with the dukedom of Burgundy	1789: National movement against Austrian Habsburg rule; September: popular uprising in Brussels; October: Belgian rebels defeat Austrians; proclamation of the United States of Belgium
1384: Philip acquires county Burgundy (Franche Comté) and Flanders	1790: Open conflict in Belgian national movement; democrats flee to Paris; November: Austrians re-occupy southern Netherlands
1430s: Philip the Good acquires Brabant, Limburg, Holland and Picardy	1792: April: Revolutionary France declares war on Austria and Prussia
	1794: French conquest of the southern Netherlands

1451: Philip the Good acquires Luxembourg	1795 – 1815: Belgian Netherlands annexed to France
1467-77: Charles the Bold adds Lorraine and Gelderland to his territories	1815–30: Belgian Netherlands incorporated in the Kingdom of the United Netherlands
1477: Charles killed in battle; the Netherlands pass to the Habsburg dynasty	1820s: Cockerill family develops industrial complex at Seraing works near Liège, using British technology; first manufacturer of steam engines in Continental Europe; steam power applied to winding coal on the Belgian coalfield; rapid development of mechanised cotton spinning in Ghent
1555: Charles V of Spain, Holy Roman Emperor and duke of Burgundy abdicates; succeeded by Philip II	1828–30: National movement against Dutch rule
1562 onwards: Inquisition in the Netherlands adopts increasingly stringent measure against Protestant heretics	1830: Uprising in Brussels; Dutch troops fire on protesting crowd in Antwerp. November; Provisional Government and National Congress declare independence
1566: mass Calvinist hedge preaching followed by iconoclastic destruction of Catholic imagery; beginnings of the first Dutch Revolt	1831: January: London Conference of great powers recognises Belgium's independence and guarantees state's perpetual neutrality; June: Belgian Constitution adopted and crown offered to Leopold of Saxe-Coburg; August: Dutch invasion of Belgium; France and Britain resort to military action to expel Dutch
1567–1572: duke of Alva, governor-general of the Netherlands: seeks to extirpate heresy and crush the revolt	1835: first steam railway opened in Belgium; basic railway network completed by 1842
1578 onwards: duke of Parma restores Spanish rule in the southern provinces and confirms the rights and privileges of the provincial Estates	1839: Treaty of London: the great powers re-affirm Belgian independence and perpetual neutrality and agree the state's modern borders
1579: northern provinces sign Union of Utrecht	
1581: United Provinces declare independence	
1584: Parma captures Antwerp; mass Calvinist migration from southern Netherlands to United Provinces; beginnings of the Counter Reformation in the south	

1714: Peace of Utrecht ends the War of the
Spanish Succession and confirms the
transfer of the southern Netherlands to the
Austrian Habsburgs

EXERCISE

Let's begin with a simple exercise which will, I hope, dispel possible sources of confusion. Write down what you understand by these proper names: *'Burgundy'* (or in French 'Bourgogne'), *'the Netherlands'* (in Dutch/Flemish 'de Nederlanden', in French 'Les Pays-Bas') and *'the United Provinces'*. Where are they located on a modern map and in relation to today's political borders? Where would they have been located on a map of Europe around 1460? You can find Burgundy by downloading a map of France from http://www.map-of-france.co.uk.

SPECIMEN ANSWER

Nowadays, 'Burgundy' refers to an administrative region of east central France, grouping together the departments of Yonne, Nièvre, Côte-d'Or and Saône-et-Loire. The administrative capital is Dijon and the Swiss border lies about 150 kilometres to the east.

'The Netherlands' these days refers to a small kingdom, with its capital at The Hague, located between Germany to the east and Belgium to the south, with what on the map looks like a pendant of territory, around Maastricht, hanging off the south east corner.

Turning the historical clock back to *c.*1460, we find these names referring to different territorial and political entities. At that date, 'the Netherlands' referred to the loose federation of seventeen provinces straddling the estuaries of the Scheldt and the Rhine; even after the United Provinces seceded, 'the Netherlands' included the southern, Habsburg provinces. In 1460, Burgundian territory extended far beyond Burgundy proper, including lands in the Low Countries and northern France.

DISCUSSION

You won't find 'the United Provinces' on a modern map but you should recall from Unit 8, that it was the name of the seven provinces which successfully rebelled against the Spanish Habsburgs and formed the Dutch Republic. (Because Holland was the richest and most populous province, English-speakers got into the bad habit of calling the Dutch state 'Holland'.)

As you will remember from Unit 2, 'Burgundy' was the name both of a duchy on the west bank of the river Saône, whose rulers were vassals of the king France *and* of a county on the east bank whose rulers were vassals of the Holy Roman Emperor. Dijon then lay much closer to the border of the French kingdom, with the two Burgundies straddling the border. The medieval county of Burgundy (sometimes known as Franche-Comté) is now part of France: if you look at a modern map, you will see the administrative region of Franche-Comté in eastern France on the border with Switzerland. From the map of 'Valois Burgundy' in Unit 2, you will see the full extent of the duke's lands, which included most of what is now Belgium, The Netherlands and Luxembourg, as well as Picardy in Northern France. But it is worth noting one enclave in the Netherlands which was not ruled by the dukes of Burgundy: the prince bishopric of Liège.

EXERCISE
From Unit 2, you learnt that historians have debated whether the Burgundian lands should be considered a state around 1460. For the sake of argument, let us call them an 'emerging' state: an aggregation of territories under a single lawful ruler with the potential to become a permanent political entity.

1   What, from the map, was the obvious difference between this aggregation and a modern state, such as Belgium?

2   How had this aggregation come into being?

3   What held it together?

4   What were the main, and again very obvious, differences between the process of aggregating the Burgundian lands and the process of constituting the Belgian state?

5   How did the status of the new Belgian monarch compare with that of the dukes of Burgundy?

6   Both the dukes of Burgundy and the Belgian monarch had to deal with representative assemblies: how would you characterise these institutions and their relationship with the ruler?

SPECIMEN ANSWER

1   The obvious difference was that the Burgundian lands were not one continuously bounded territory. Even after Charles the Bold had acquired Lorraine, a thirty mile gap separated his northern and southern territories. Most modern states, such as Belgium, are continuously bounded territories, and do not tolerate enclaves of another ruler's territory within their borders (which the dukes of Burgundy did.)

2   The origins of the Burgundian aggregation lay in the marriage, in the 1380s, of Philip the Bold to Margaret of Male, the heiress to the Count of Flanders, who had dynastic claims to neighbouring territories.

3   They and their heirs acquired other territories by purchase and conquest, but the principal 'glue' holding the Burgundian lands together was the ruler's personal legitimacy.

4   There was an obvious temporal difference in that, while the Burgundian lands were aggregated by their rulers over several generations, modern Belgium was constituted during a few months in 1830–31. The new state originated in a popular uprising against Dutch rule. The National Congress – acting in the name of the sovereign people – drew up a constitution and invited a German prince, Leopold of Saxe-Coburg, to rule as a constitutional monarch. His legitimacy derived in theory from the people's sovereignty: note that he was king of *the Belgians*, not king of Belgium.

5   As a sovereign, Leopold enjoyed equal status with other European sovereigns and owed homage to none. The dukes of Burgundy, though comparatively far more powerful in their territories, did not have sovereign status: they held ducal Burgundy and Picardy as vassals of the king of France and Franche-Comté and the Netherlands as vassals of the Holy Roman Emperor.

6   To raise taxes, the Valois dukes of Burgundy had to secure the consent of the various *Estates* in the territories over which they ruled. Estates were so called because they represented the social estates, that is, the clergy, nobility and burghers. When assembled, delegates from the three social estates usually sat separately. In the Netherlands each province had its own Estates (confusingly,

they are also called 'States' in the English-language historiography). The Estates General of the Netherlands referred to in Unit 2 was created by Philip the Good to simplify the process of putting fiscal demands to his subjects. The tripling of taxation between his reign and that of Charles the Bold suggests to me that the dukes could normally overawe the Estates General, but note how the latter's power increased when Charles's death left the Burgundian patrimony vulnerable. In February 1477, the Estates General wrung from his daughter, Mary, the Great Privilege, the first constitution for the entire Netherlands. As you will have gathered from Unit 8, the Habsburg dukes were also obliged to convene the Estates General to raise taxes, but they frustrated any attempt on the assembly's part to represent the entire Netherlands and eventually annulled the Great Privilege.

You are not told much about the Belgian parliament, but enough to gather that it was the real centre of power in a parliamentary monarchy. (It is worth adding here – though you cannot be expected to know this – that the Chamber of Deputies was elected on a franchise restricted to men owning substantial property. In 1848, the franchise was broadened to 'head off' the revolutionary contagion emanating from France; in 1894, universal male suffrage was introduced following a general strike.)

EXERCISE

Political *representation* is a key concept in analysing the form taken by the state in any era. In this regard, Burgundy and Belgium are an instructive pairing because the former was typical of fifteenth-century states in Latin Christendom and the latter of nineteenth-century constitutional states. So how would you characterise and contrast representation in the late medieval and modern liberal state?

SPECIMEN ANSWER

The function of the Estates in Valois Burgundy was to represent the ascribed status groups of a hierarchical social order; that is to say, representation was corporate (or corporatist). The function of the Belgian Chamber of Deputies was to represent the individual citizens who made up the sovereign people.

DISCUSSION

So why wasn't the Chamber elected on a democratic male franchise when the state was constituted? The bourgeois Liberals and Catholics who dominated the revolution of 1830–31 considered – like middle-class liberals throughout Europe at this time – that only men of some economic substance had the necessary independence to exercise their political judgement without fear or favour, and so accepted the need for a property qualification for the franchise. It was the duty of the better off to ensure the *virtual representation* of the poor. More men would be enfranchised as economic growth led to the generalisation of prosperity – which we could call the 'trickle down' theory of democratisation. The Belgian Liberals considered religious belief a private matter and irrelevant to the public sphere of the state, so they enfranchised Jews, provided they met the property qualification. (Jewish emancipation is a good index of liberal state formation: American Jews were granted full civil and political rights during the War of Independence, French Jews in 1791, British Jews in 1858, German Jews in 1871 with the formation of the Second Empire, though some German states had previously emancipated Jews.)

EXERCISE

This next exercise should make you think about the relationship between religious affiliation and political/national frontiers. Did religious denomination determine the national border between modern Belgium and The Netherlands? Or had religious denomination, especially in the south, been determined by the historic border between the United Provinces and the Habsburg provinces?

SPECIMEN ANSWER

The answer to both questions is a qualified 'Yes but ...'

DISCUSSION

The religious factor had *some* significance in the Belgian revolution of 1830–31, for the Belgians – who greatly outnumbered the Dutch – were overwhelmingly Catholic (as they still are). The Dutch were predominantly Protestant, though with a substantial Catholic minority. Although William I had kept the promise made in 1815 to respect freedom of worship, southerners disliked the sectarian influence of the Dutch Reformed Church on William's government. Distrust of the government was especially evident in Flanders, where most schools were run by the Catholic Church and the clergy enjoyed considerable esteem. But the Belgian national movement brought progressive Flemish Catholics into uncomfortable alliance with Liberal Walloons who were *anti-clerical* and advocated a state monopoly of education. The common Catholic–Liberal programme demanded press freedom and electoral reform to give the southern province fair representation in parliament, where over half the seats were reserved for 'Dutch' constituencies. The border finally agreed by the Dutch and Belgian governments in 1839 followed the old frontier of the United Provinces, except for the south eastern pendant which had not been part of the Dutch Republic (although the city of Maastricht had). In the east, the frontier was fixed by partitioning the duchy of Luxembourg – which the Orange family ruled as hereditary dukes – between Belgium and William. The personal union between Luxembourg and The Netherlands was dissolved in 1890, when William III died without a male heir.

It is tempting to project the Catholic homogeneity of the Belgian Netherlands back into the later sixteenth century and assume that this determined the frontier with the United Provinces, but that would be a mistake. It is more true to say that the political frontier determined that all who lived to the south conformed to Catholicism. This conformity could not have been anticipated in the 1560s when popular disaffection from the Roman Church was as evident in the southern as in the northern provinces.

You will recall from Unit 8 that Calvinist hedge preaching began in Flanders and Brabant before spreading to Holland and Zeeland. In August 1566, most southern towns were engulfed by a wave of anti-Catholic iconoclasm; every Catholic church in Antwerp was ransacked and stripped of its images, paintings and revered objects. The re-conquest of the south by Spanish Habsburg forces in 1584–85 led first to the mass exodus of irreconcilable Protestants (about half Antwerp's population moved north after the city was recaptured by the Duke of Parma) and later to strenuous efforts to win back hearts and minds for the Catholic Church. The Counter Reformation had some of its most striking successes in the southern Netherlands: by 1630, Protestantism had disappeared from Antwerp and other southern cities. This was not simply a matter of the Church acting as the spiritual arm of an all-powerful state: missionary priests who were allowed into the southern border region of the United Provinces had considerable success reconverting the people to Catholicism. The confessional boundaries which emerged in the Low Countries in the early seventeenth century have persisted ever since. They do not coincide with political boundaries: when the Belgian provinces seceded in 1830–31, the southern border region of what is now The Netherlands was overwhelmingly Catholic. But there was no hint of the Dutch Catholics wishing to join their co-religionists in the new Belgian state. National identity was a more compelling component of political consciousness than confession.

Yet over the centuries there had been a loose and reciprocal relationship between religion, state formation and political frontiers: the territorial entity with which the Belgian nationalists identified was delimited by the military stalemate between the Habsburgs and the United Provinces, and religious differences had inspired the Dutch revolt. The Belgians' allegiance to Catholicism clearly owed much to the restoration of Habsburg state power south of the strategically-determined frontier with the United Provinces. When I referred to the 'articulation' of political geography with religious beliefs it was this loose and reciprocal relationship I had in mind.

EXERCISE

What was the historic watershed separating states aggregated over many decades by dynastic aggrandisement and states constituted by a deliberate act of a national assembly? What political beliefs and ideologies lay behind this watershed?

SPECIMEN ANSWER

The watershed is conventionally taken to be the French Revolution (Unit 17). If we wanted to be precise it was the moment (20 June 1789) when the Third Estate – which had declared itself the National Assembly – took a collective oath not to disband until the constitution was adopted. But you will recall from Block 4 a significant precedent in the constitution of the United States of America in September 1787. Because the American example closely preceded and greatly influenced the French revolutionaries, some historians have taken the historic watershed to have been the era of 'Atlantic' or 'democratic' revolution. The political beliefs and ideologies behind this watershed were the concept of *popular sovereignty*, meaning legitimate and untrammelled power derived from the people, and the modern concept of the *nation* as a political community entitled to express itself in a state, which gave rise to the idea of the *nation state*. If we concentrate on the American Constitution, we find embedded in it the ideas of the *separation of powers*, the *secularisation* of the state, and formal *social equality*. The Constitution prohibits any religious 'establishment' – or state religion – and titles of nobility. The French revolutionaries followed the American example by disestablishing the Catholic Church and stripping the aristocracy of its corporate rights and privileges and introducing the concept of *citizenship*, a status accorded to all adult men in the sovereign nation. They also paid lip service to the ideal of the separation of powers, though in the crisis years of 1793–94, legislative, executive and judicial powers were fused in the Committee of Public Safety.

DISCUSSION

Paris was not the only European capital in revolutionary ferment in 1789. In Brussels, a proto-nationalist movement had coalesced against the reforming policies of the Austrian Emperor Joseph II. It had two contradictory components: one was the conservative defence of provincial rights and privileges which Joseph sought to curtail; the other was the demand for popular sovereignty on American lines. Early in the year, the national symbol of modern Belgium – the tricolour flag of red, yellow and black – was invented when a brewer painted the door of his house with the colours of Brabant. The term 'Belgians' was adopted to embrace both Flemish and French speakers, a sign that the politically active were recognising each other as belonging to the same nation *despite* differences in language and cultural traditions. The Austrian regime collapsed in October1789, after Belgian rebels who had assembled in the United Provinces invaded. The Estates General of the southern Netherlands, which has not met since 1634, reconvened itself. In the following months, each province separately declared its independence. Their representatives created the United States of Belgium with a legal instrument closely modelled on the American Articles of Confederation. A federal government was established, with powers carefully limited to foreign policy and defence. The revolution's contradictory components soon became openly hostile: the staunchly Catholic burgher elites who dominated the provincial Estates and Estates General desired simply to exclude the Austrians and maintain the particular rights and privileges they had wrested from the dukes of Burgundy; but the 'democrats' – as they called themselves – advocated a 'Jacobin' programme of political and civil reforms. (This was the first use of the word 'democrat' in political discourse in the Euro-American world.) The conservative 'Statists' gained the upper hand by inciting Catholic mobs to lynch democrats, who were unfairly accused of planning to nationalise the Church and sequester its property. Those who could fled to Paris, where they became vocal proponents of the liberation of Belgium by the revolution in arms.

Austrian forces re-occupied the southern Netherlands in November 1790, but what really extinguished the first Belgian state was the military expansion of revolutionary France. With the French declaration of war on Austria and Prussia in April 1792, the southern Low Countries were inevitably going to be a key military theatre and a major political stake in the conflict. The region had been the strategic cockpit of Western Europe since the later sixteenth century; the emergence of a militantly nationalist France could only enhance its geopolitical importance. The 'war party' in the French National Assembly argued that the nation's 'natural frontiers' were the Rhine and the Alps and demanded the annexation of foreign territories within these frontiers. While political rhetoric proclaimed the revolutionary fraternity of all sovereign peoples, national policy was brutally chauvinist. Following the crushing victory over the Austrians at Fleurus (June, 1794), Belgium was formally annexed to France in October 1795. Sweeping institutional change followed: the old provincial administration was replaced by nine departments and the French judicial system introduced. The religious orders were suppressed and their buildings and property were confiscated. The peasants gained free-hold title to the land they tilled and vestigial feudal constraints were abolished.

EXERCISE

Let's now tease out the connections between economic modernisation, nationalism and the formation of the Belgian nation state. First, summarise in your own words Gellner's thesis (from your work on Unit 19) as to the relationship between nationalism and economic modernity, then say if the information provided so far validates his thesis.

SPECIMEN ANSWER

1   Gellner argued that nation-states are intrinsically modern and only became possible with the transition from agrarian to industrial society, which entailed greater geographic and social mobility and 'portable' social relations. In agrarian society, culture was horizontally stratified: only a tiny minority were literate and the ruling elite spoke a different language and espoused different values from those of the common people.

The case of Valois Burgundy offers a good illustration of this: its French-speaking courtly culture was a world apart from the popular culture of the Flemish countryside and small towns. Industrial society could not function without vertical cultural links between employers and employed and rulers and ruled. To create a common, literate and accessible culture, modern industrial states invested in education systems and made schooling compulsory. By gaining a monopoly over education (and by imposing a national curriculum), states thereby *created* nations (rather than the other way around). Nationalism – Gellner concluded – was an essential component of modernisation, but it was not the awakening of nations to self-consciousness; rather states invented nations where they did not exist.

2   Belgium was the first country in Continental Europe to industrialise and became one of the world's most industrialised economies. So it should provide an interesting test of Gellner's argument. However, the first, aborted national revolution (of 1789–90) preceded the onset of industrialisation by about a quarter of a century. National identity was formed in opposition to an Austrian ruler who was felt to be intruding on traditional rights and privileges; it was, partly, a *re-active* sentiment, though emulation of the Americans was also significant. The nation was scarcely 'invented' by the state, though the sovereign people were invoked by the conservative Estates when constituting the Union. The dense, urban culture had an ambiguous relationship with national identity and nation state formation: towns and cities were centres of opposition to Austrian rule but their civic elites clung to the historic rights and privileges of the provincial Estates, which frustrated the development of modern state institutions. These were imposed from outside.

DISCUSSION

At first blush, then, economic modernisation appears to have had some connection with the second, successful national revolution, but was industrialisation served by seceding from the United Netherlands? And why didn't *this* state create a common Netherlands culture to accommodate the industrial society emerging in its southern provinces? One element of a common culture was present because Dutch was widely spoken in the south, but this was insufficient to reconcile Flemish Catholics to a monarchy they perceived as sectarian. Gellner's theory assumed that nationalism would accompany cultural secularisation, but the Belgian example shows that nationalism and confessional solidarity could complement each other (as they have in other 'small nations', such as Catholic Ireland, Catholic Croatia, Orthodox Serbia). Of course, a proponent of Gellner's theory could maintain that the Belgian nation was really 'invented' by the mid-nineteenth-century liberal state to hold together its language communities and antagonistic social classes. But the evidence is not that persuasive because the state left so much of popular education to the Church, which made a poor job of it. In 1900, about 15 per cent of Belgian children did not go to school and nearly one in five of the population over 8 years could neither read nor write.

It is arguable that Belgian nationalism, and the formation of a Belgian nation state, ran counter to the 'logic' of Belgian industrialisation. The owners of the newly mechanising industries (who were mostly Walloons) gained real advantages from the large market formed by The United Netherlands. The Dutch were very slow to industrialise so they did not compete with southern manufacturers, but they consumed Belgian cotton goods, iron-ware and steam-wound coal. The Dutch East Indies were an important colonial market for Belgian cottons. William's government positively encouraged southern industrialisation by placing government orders with Walloon industrialists and granting subsidies. Dutch investment flowed into the Société générale, founded in Brussels in 1822, which became the core financial institution of the modern Belgian economy. Furthermore, the creation of the United Netherlands had definitively opened the Scheldt to maritime shipping and permitted the rapid development of Antwerp's entrepôt trade.[3] Most Belgian businessmen wanted to maintain William's sovereignty, in order to safeguard the economic unity of the Low Countries, while securing greater administrative and financial autonomy for the Belgian provinces. Strident economic nationalism was voiced only by those producers (manufacturers of cotton yarn, hand-loom weavers) who sought greater tariff protection from British competition. The national revolution certainly drew upon socio-economic grievances in the textiles industry, which was facing a severe slump in the spring of 1830, but it was first and foremost a political movement. Its most prominent leaders were lawyers and journalists who aimed to create a state which Belgians – more particularly the bourgeoisie – would regard as legitimate.

EXERCISE

The Belgian case bears out Breuilly's dictum that we must seek the explanation for nationalism in the political context and elite politics. But there is one aspect of 'the political context' not mentioned in Unit 19 which was clearly crucial to the *success* of the Belgian national revolution, and was a major variable in determining nation-state formation throughout the nineteenth-century. What was that 'aspect?'

SPECIMEN ANSWER

It was the *international* political context, more specifically the balance of power in the 'system' of major sovereign states.

DISCUSSION

This point is worth expanding on because it demonstrates how small nation states were formed in a continent dominated by five great powers (three autocratic states: Russia, Austria and Prussia, and liberal Britain and France). The Belgian bid for independence was a breach the Vienna settlement of 1815, which had been intended to contain France and the revolutionary threat associated with France. William appealed (as was his right) to the great powers for assistance in suppressing the rebellion. Russia and Prussia were ready to aid the Dutch government with troops but Britain and France were determined to resist this. To avert the looming crisis, the British government proposed an international conference to settle the 'Belgian question'. British interests largely determined its outcome. French nationalists had pressed for the annexation of the Walloon provinces, to which the British government was fiercely opposed, and Louis-Philippe's government wisely resisted their demands. In January, the London conference recognised the new state's independence and guaranteed its perpetual neutrality. It also decided that no candidate for the Belgian crown could be chosen from the ruling dynasty of any of the great powers. This clause was intended to block the candidacy of one of Louis-Philippe's sons, for whom there was strong support in the Belgian Constituent Assembly. The British government bluntly told Louis-Philippe that it would resort to immediate war to prevent any future union of the French and Belgian monarchies;

---

[3] In 1585, the United Provinces had won control of the Scheldt estuary and insisted on closing it to maritime trade. Under the Peace of Münster (1648), which brought the 'Eighty Years' War' to an end, Spain agreed to the perpetual closure of the Scheldt.

on 17 February he withdrew his son's candidacy. Some Belgian aristocrats wanted to maintain the link with The Netherlands by offering the crown to the Prince of Orange, but he was totally unacceptable to the clergy and the mass of the people. In June, Leopold of Saxe-Coburg accepted the crown from the National Congress. That was not the end of the 'Belgian question', or of the 'shaping' of the Belgian state by the international states system. The Dutch king rejected the decisions of the London conference and ordered an invasion of Belgium in August; Antwerp was captured and the Scheldt blockaded by the Dutch navy. Both Britain and France intervened militarily to assist Belgium: at Leopold's request, the French sent an army across Belgium to drive the Dutch out of Antwerp and the British navy blockaded the Dutch coast to compel the Dutch to lift their own blockade of the Scheldt. William's intransigence led to a less favourable territorial settlement for his family than the London conference had agreed, because Britain and France now supported Belgian claims to the eastern part of the duchy of Luxembourg. William stubbornly resisted acknowledging political realities until April 1839, when he, and all the major powers, signed the Treaty of London, which re-affirmed Belgium's independence and perpetual neutrality.

So how would we summarily explain Belgian state formation? Popular nationalism was *a necessary but not a sufficient* condition. The state came into being as a British–French protectorate and its independence and status were recognised by international treaty. The Belgian 'success story' can be instructively contrasted with the failed nationalist insurrection in 1830–31 in Congress Poland, the rump state created in 1815 where the Russian Tsar ruled as a constitutional monarch. Polish national patriotism had deeper historical roots than Belgian nationalism for the Poles were clearly one of Europe's historic nations, with a vibrant national culture, an intelligentsia expressing itself in one literary language, and the most determined of all national movements, which enjoyed the support of the Catholic clergy. *But all this did not suffice to create a Polish nation-state.* That depended on the revolution in the international states system brought about by the First World War. In a not dissimilar war, the end of the Cold War and the fall of communism have permitted the emergence of a rash of new (or revived) nation-states.

Finally, let's tease out the relationship between the liberal constitutional state formed in Belgium in 1830–31 and the industrialising society emerging in its towns and villages. The class character of the state was patent: the bourgeoisie or urban upper middle classes monopolised political power through the restriction of the franchise to wealthy taxpayers, many of whom had plural voting rights. Prior to the electoral reform of 1848, there were about 60,000 voters in a population of 4.7 million. Class domination was not 'pure'; it intermeshed with, and was modified by other types of social division. Flanders, especially the over-populated countryside, was poorer and its people more inward-looking, less literate and less entrepreneurial than the Walloons. In Brussels, the language divide tended to reinforce class divisions: French-speaking households commonly employed Flemish servants, for example, but Walloon servants rarely worked for Flemish mistresses. Elsewhere, language communities tended to cut across social classes because educated French-speakers were usually anti-clerical and middle-class Flemings strongly Catholic. Until the later nineteenth century, the working class stood passively by while the Catholic and Liberal parties contested the limited political terrain. In terms of their constituencies and political ideologies, they were both bourgeois parties. What divided them was the question of the clerical control of education.

To historians, working-class passivity has seemed especially puzzling in 1848 – the year of revolutions elsewhere – when Belgium was gripped by a protracted social crisis and hundreds of thousands of workers were on public relief. The crisis had two dimensions: one was agrarian distress of familiar kind following harvest failure. The famine in rural Flanders, where the potato crop failed in successive years, was comparable to that in Ireland. The other dimension was quite novel: massive industrial unemployment following a recession and a wave of bankruptcies. Explanations as to why the Belgian state weathered this dire social crisis with comparative ease focus on the deft political manoeuvring of the Liberal Party, which won an absolute majority in the Chamber of Deputies in 1847. The government disarmed its lower middle-class critics by reforming the tax system, abolishing the tax on newspapers, prohibiting office holding by deputies (a measure intended to curb political corruption) and broadening the franchise, though only a further 20,000 were added to the electoral rolls. Public works were organised to assist the unemployed and destitute. The borders were sealed at the outbreak of the February revolution in Paris and the radical exiles congregating in Brussels were expelled. But the roots of working-class passivity seem to have lain more deeply in the pattern of workers' lives: illiteracy was much higher in Brussels and Antwerp than in Paris or Lyons; there was no working-class press and little tradition of workers' organisation or education. The common practice in industrial workers' families of retaining a small-holding, usually worked by a wife while her wage-earning husband commuted to the mill, mine or forge, kept the working class half in the rural world.

Universal male suffrage came late to Belgium (as it did to Britain) and far from being a 'natural' outgrowth of the liberal constitutional state, it was conceded only after workers had organised and taken industrial action. The emergence of a labour movement which bridged the language barrier was delayed until 1885, when the Belgian Labour Party was formed through the amalgamation of Flemish and Walloon socialist parties. In the following year, a socialist pamphlet demanding universal suffrage provoked a great and largely spontaneous strike movement in the Belgian coal-field. The government responded, as it had to earlier miners' strikes, by proclaiming martial law and using troops to guard the factories and pit-heads and clear the streets of demonstrators. The draconian crack-down broke the strike and was followed by the exemplary prosecution of its leaders: some were sentenced to twenty years' solitary confinement. This set-back led to much factional dispute within the Labour Party over the appropriate tactics to follow in pursuit of manhood suffrage. The proponents of direct action won the argument, and the party called a national general strike in May 1892, which compelled Parliament to convene a constituent assembly to discuss electoral reform. But the elections (on the existing franchise) were won by the Catholic Party, which opposed universal suffrage. So the Labour Party called another general strike in early 1893. This persuaded the parliamentarians to pass a Reform Act which multiplied the electorate tenfold, but retained plural voting rights which gave the middle classes a built-in advantage in elections to the Chamber of Deputies. The Labour Party made significant gains under the new electoral law, but continued to militate for an equal franchise. In early 1902, the party called once more for a general strike and secured further changes in the franchise. By 1914, it represented 30 per cent of the Belgian electorate. It was one of the best-organised political parties in the world which federated trade unions, co-operative societies, and socialist and educational societies. The party helped *producers* negotiate with their employers and provided *consumers* with facilities for buying food and clothing more cheaply. It also insured them against illness, unemployment and old age, while providing medical treatment and opportunities for recreation and education. It represented an embryonic welfare state.

The party endorsed the principle of female suffrage – in line with social democratic parties throughout Europe – but its leaders' public reservations made this commitment virtually meaningless. One notoriously declared that women were not yet intellectually mature enough to be given political rights. The charitable explanation for this fatuous pronouncement is visceral anti-clericalism: women were thought to be more susceptible to priestly influence and more likely to vote for the Catholic parties, which by the late 1890s were actively courting workers' votes. After the First World War, the vote was granted to war widows and the mothers of fallen sons – women who had the privilege of representing dead men. Full adult suffrage was not enacted until 1948.

CODA

Belgium is a small country: an energetic pair on a tandem can cross from France to The Netherlands in a day, though they would have to be pretty attentive to notice the borders these days. Much more evident is the linguistic frontier between language communities, seemingly there to confuse foreign cyclists. Yet, within its narrow compass, Belgium experienced the manifold transformations from medieval to modern in a peculiarly concentrated way. Brussels and Ghent were the centres of the northern Renaissance and Burgundy's great high culture. The Reformation and Counter-Reformation surged back and forth across the southern Netherlands, as did political revolution and counter-revolution after 1789. Belgium was the classic example of the liberal constitutional state, and one of the earliest centres of industrial capitalism. In the early twentieth century, it became the most unlikely of the modern imperial powers. No country less deserves the epithet 'boring'.

INDEX